Selected Letters of
Abigail and John Adams

SELECTED LETTERS OF ABIGAIL AND JOHN ADAMS

Abigail and John Adams

DOVER PUBLICATIONS, INC.
GARDEN CITY, NEW YORK

DOVER THRIFT EDITIONS

GENERAL EDITOR: SUSAN L. RATTINER
EDITOR OF THIS VOLUME: MICHAEL CROLAND

Bibliographical Note

This Dover edition, first published in 2021, is a new selection of letters reprinted from standard texts. The letters were written by Abigail and John Adams between March 1776 and March 1777. Misspellings, minor inconsistencies, and other style vagaries derive from the original texts and have been retained for the sake of authenticity. A new introductory Note has been specially prepared for this edition.

Library of Congress Cataloging-in-Publication Data

Names: Adams, Abigail, 1744–1818, author. | Adams, John, 1735–1826, author.
Title: Selected letters of Abigail and John Adams / Abigail and John Adams.
Description: Garden City, New York : Dover Publications, Inc., 2021. | Series: Dover thrift editions | Summary: "Abigail and John Adams exchanged more than 1,000 letters. Their lively correspondence offers fascinating insights into domestic and public life in colonial and post-Revolutionary America"— Provided by publisher.
Identifiers: LCCN 2020035384 | ISBN 9780486841700 (trade paperback)
Subjects: LCSH: Adams, John, 1735–1826—Correspondence. | Adams, Abigail, 1744–1818—Correspondence. | Married people—United States— Correspondence. | United States—History—Revolution, 1775–1783— Sources. | United States—History—1783–1815—Sources. | American letters. | Adams family.
Classification: LCC E322 .A4 2021 | DDC 973.4/40922—dc23
LC record available at https://lccn.loc.gov/2020035384

Manufactured in the United States by LSC Communications
84170701
www.doverpublications.com

2 4 6 8 10 9 7 5 3 1

2021

Note

JOHN AND ABIGAIL ADAMS were the premier power couple of the revolutionary era.

John Adams was born in Braintree, Massachusetts, in 1735. He graduated from Harvard College and worked as a lawyer. He was a revered political philosopher and a delegate to the First and Second Continental Congresses. He served as a diplomat in France and Holland during the Revolutionary War and helped negotiate the peace treaty. He was the nation's first ambassador to Great Britain and first vice president. In 1797, he became the second president of the United States.

Abigail Smith was born in Weymouth, Massachusetts, in 1744. She was homeschooled, benefiting from the extensive library of her father, a minister, as well as frequent visits from well-educated guests. As first lady, she frequently discussed political matters, which was not commonplace for that role until the twentieth century.

Adams and Smith met in 1759, when he was twenty-four and she was going on fifteen. During their first ten years of marriage, they had five children, including future president John Quincy Adams. For much of their second decade as husband and wife, John was away, either as a member of the Continental Congress or representing the nascent country abroad. When he traveled, Abigail managed his business affairs and the family's farm.

The couple exchanged more than 1,000 letters beginning in 1761. The letters depict their love and their view of each other as intellectual equals. Abigail signs some of her letters "Portia," a nickname that John gave her, likely after the heroine in William Shakespeare's *The Merchant of Venice*.

While John claimed that the letters were originally meant for his family and not a wider contemporary audience, historians believe that the Adamses wanted them to be saved for posterity. In 1776, John bought a sturdy binder to store Abigail's letters and encouraged her to follow suit. John appreciated the scope and significance of the collection when he reread the letters later in life. He set up an archive and hired editors to go through them.

"The sheer emotional power of it and the literary sophistication of it is so overwhelming," noted historian Joseph J. Ellis. He said that the abundant letters present "a great story" that is "a love story." Ellis explained that because John and Abigail were frequently apart, there were more opportunities for letters.

The present volume features eighty-one letters ranging from March 1776 to March 1777. Among the topics discussed are reflections on government, Congress's creation of the Board of War and Ordnance, Congress's vote for independence and approval of the Declaration of Independence, Abigail Adams's visit to Boston with the couple's children and servants for smallpox inoculation, and John Adams's trip to New York with Benjamin Franklin and Edward Rutledge to meet with British peace commissioners.

SELECTED LETTERS OF ABIGAIL AND JOHN ADAMS

1. Abigail Adams

I WAS GREATLY rejoiced at the return of your servant, to find you had safely arrived, and that you were well. I had never heard a word from you after you had left New York, and a most ridiculous story had been industriously propagated in this and the neighboring towns to injure the cause and blast your reputation; namely, that you and your President had gone on board of a man-of-war from New York, and sailed for England. I should not mention so idle a report, but that it had given uneasiness to some of your friends; not that they in the least credited the report, but because the gaping vulgar swallowed the story. One man had deserted them and proved a traitor, another might, etc. I assure you, such high disputes took place in the public-house of this parish, that some men were collared and dragged out of the shop with great threats, for reporting such scandalous lies, and an uncle of ours offered his life as a forfeit for you, if the report proved true. However, it has been a nine days' marvel, and will now cease. I heartily wish every Tory was extirpated from America; they are continually, by secret means, undermining and injuring our cause.

I am charmed with the sentiments of "Common Sense," and wonder how an honest heart, one who wishes the welfare of his country and the happiness of posterity, can hesitate one moment at adopting them. I want to know how these sentiments are received in Congress. I dare say there would be no difficulty in procuring a vote and instructions from all the Assemblies in New England for Independency. I most sincerely wish that now, in the lucky minute, it might be done.

I have been kept in a continual state of anxiety and expectation ever since you left me. It has been said "to-morrow" and "to-morrow," for this month, but when the dreadful to-morrow will be, I know not. But hark! The house this instant shakes with the roar of cannon. I have been to the door, and find it is a cannonade from our army. Orders, I find, are come for all the remaining militia to repair to the lines Monday night by twelve o'clock. No sleep for me to-night. And if I cannot, who have no guilt upon my soul with regard to this cause, how shall the miserable wretches who have been the procurers of this dreadful scene, and those who are to be the actors, lie down with the load of guilt upon their souls?

Sunday Evening, 3 March

I went to bed after twelve, but got no rest; the cannon continued firing, and my heart beat pace with them all night. We have had a pretty quiet day, but what to-morrow will bring forth, God only knows.

Monday Evening

Tolerable quiet. To-day the militia have all mustered, with three days' provision, and are all marched by three o'clock this afternoon, though their notice was no longer ago than eight o'clock, Saturday. And now we have scarcely a man, but our regular guards, either in Weymouth, Hingham, Braintree, or Milton, and the militia from the more remote towns are called in as seacoast guards. Can you form to yourself an idea of our sensations? Palmer is chief colonel, Bass is lieutenant-colonel, and Soper major and Hall captain.

I have just returned from Penn's Hill, where I have been sitting to hear the amazing roar of cannon, and from whence I could see every shell which was thrown. The sound, I think, is one of the grandest in nature, and is of the true species of the sublime. 'Tis now an incessant roar; but oh! the fatal ideas which are connected with the sound! How many of our dear countrymen must fall!

Tuesday Morning

I went to bed about twelve, and rose again a little after one. I could no more sleep than if I had been in the engagement; the rattling of the windows, the jar of the house, the continual roar of twenty-four pounders, and the bursting of shells, give us such ideas, and realize a scene to us of which we could form scarcely any conception. About six, this morning, there was quiet. I rejoiced in a few hours' calm. I hear we got possession of Dorchester Hill last night; four thousand men upon it to-day; lost but one man. The ships are all drawn round the town. To-night we shall realize a more terrible scene still. I sometimes think I cannot stand it. I wish myself with you, out of hearing, as I cannot assist them. I hope to give you joy of Boston, even if it is in ruins, before I send this away. I am too much agitated to write as I ought, and languid for want of rest.

Thursday, Fast-day

All my anxiety and distress is at present at an end. I feel disappointed. This day our militia are all returning without effecting anything more than taking possession of Dorchester Hill. I hope it is wise and just, but, from all the muster and stir, I hoped and expected more important and decisive scenes. I would not have suffered all I have for two such hills. Ever since the taking of that, we have had a perfect calm; nor can I learn yet what effect it has had in Boston. I do not hear of one person's escaping since.

I was very much pleased with your choice of a committee for Canada. All those to whom I have ventured to show that part of your letter, approve the scheme of the priest as a master-stroke of policy. I feel sorry that General Lee has left us, but his presence at New York was no doubt of great importance, as we have reason to think it prevented Clinton from landing and gathering together such a nest of vermin as would at least have distressed us greatly. But how can you spare him from here? Can you make his place good? Can you supply it with a man equally qualified to save us? How do the Virginians relish the troops said to be destined for them? Are they putting themselves into a state of defense? I inclose to you a copy of a letter sent by Captain Furnance, who is in Mr. Ned Church's employ, and who came into the Cape about ten days ago. You will learn the sentiments of our cousin by it. Some of which may be true, but I hope he is a much better divine than politician. I hear that in one of his letters he mentions certain intercepted letters which he says have made much noise in England, and laments that you ever wrote them. I cannot bear to think of your continuing in a state of supineness this winter.

> "There is a tide in the affairs of men,
> Which, taken at the flood, leads on to fortune;
> Omitted, all the voyage of their life
> Is bound in shallows and in miseries.
> On such a full sea are we now afloat;
> And we must take the current when it serves,
> Or lose our ventures."

Sunday Evening, 10 March

I had scarcely finished these lines when my ears were again assaulted by the roar of cannon. I could not write any further. My hand and heart will tremble at this "domestic fury and fierce civil strife," which "cumber all" our "parts"; though "blood and destruction" are "so much in use," "and dreadful objects so familiar," yet is not "pity choked," nor my heart grown callous. I feel for the unhappy wretches who know not where to fly for safety. I feel still more for my bleeding countrymen, who are hazarding their lives and their limbs. A most terrible and incessant cannonade from half after eight till six this morning. I hear we lost four men killed, and some wounded, in attempting to take the hill nearest the town, called Nook's Hill. We did some work, but the fire from the ships beat off our men, so that they did not secure it, but retired to the fort upon the other hill.

I have not got all the particulars; I wish I had; but, as I have an opportunity of sending this, I shall endeavor to be more particular in my next. All our little ones send duty. Tommy has been very sick with what is called the scarlet or purple fever, but has got about again.

If there are reinforcements here, I believe we shall be driven from the seacoast; but, in whatever state I am, I will endeavor to be therewith content.

> "Man wants but little here below,
> Nor wants that little long."

You will excuse this very incorrect letter. You see in what perturbation it has been written, and how many times I have left off. Adieu.

Yours.

P.S. Took's grammar is the one you mention.

2. Abigail Adams

B——e, 16 March 1776

I LAST EVENING received yours of March 8. I was in continual expectation that some important event would take place to give me a subject worth writing upon. Before this reaches you, I imagine you will have received two letters from me; the last I closed this day week. Since that time there have been some movements amongst the ministerial troops, as if they meant to evacuate the town of Boston. Between seventy and eighty vessels of various sizes are gone down, and lie in a row in fair sight of this place, all of which appear to be loaded; and by what can be collected from our own observations, and from deserters, they have been plundering the town. I have been very faithless with regard to their quitting Boston, and know not how to account for it; nor am I yet satisfied that they will leave it, though it seems to be the prevailing opinion of most people.

We are obliged to place the militia upon guard every night upon the shores, through fear of an invasion. There has been no firing since last Tuesday till about twelve o'clock last night, when I was waked out of my sleep with a smart cannonade, which continued till nine o'clock this morning, and prevented any further repose for me. The occasion I have not yet heard; but before I close this letter I may be able to give you some account of it.

By the accounts in the public papers, the plot thickens, and some very important crisis seems near at hand. Perhaps Providence sees it necessary, in order to answer important ends and designs, that the seat of war should be changed from this to the southern colonies, that each may have a proper sympathy with the other, and unite in a separation. The refuge of the believer, amidst all the afflictive

5

dispensations of Providence, is that the Lord reigneth, and that He can restrain the arm of man.

Orders are given to our army to hold themselves in readiness to march at a moment's warning. "I'll meet you at Philippi," said the ghost of Caesar to Brutus.

Sunday Noon

Being quite sick with a violent cold, I have tarried at home to-day. I find the firing was occasioned by our people's taking possession of Nook's Hill, which they kept in spite of the cannonade, and which has really obliged our enemy to decamp this morning on board the transports, as I hear by a messenger just come from headquarters. Some of the selectmen have been to the lines, and inform that they have carried away everything they could possibly take; and what they could not, they have burnt, broke, or hove into the water. This is, I believe, fact; many articles of good household furniture having in the course of the week come on shore at Great Hill, both upon this and Weymouth side,—lids of desks, mahogany chairs, tables, etc. Our people, I hear, will have liberty to enter Boston,—those who have had the small-pox.

The enemy have not yet come under sail. I cannot help suspecting some design, which we do not yet comprehend. To what quarter of the world they are bound is wholly unknown; but 'tis generally thought to New York. Many people are elated with their quitting Boston. I confess I do not feel so. 'Tis only lifting the burden from one shoulder to the other, which is perhaps less able or less willing to support it. To what a contemptible situation are the troops of Britain reduced! I feel glad, however, that Boston is not destroyed. I hope it will be so secured and guarded as to baffle all future attempts against it. I hear that General Howe said, upon going on some eminence in town to view our troops, who had taken Dorchester Hill, unperceived by them till sunrise, "My God, these fellows have done more work in one night than I could make my army do in three months." And he might well say so; for in one night two forts and long breastworks were sprung up, besides several barracks. Three hundred and seventy teams were employed, most of which went three loads in the night, besides four thousand men, who worked with good hearts.

From Penn's Hill we have a view of the largest fleet ever seen in America. You may count upwards of a hundred and seventy sail.

They look like a forest. It was very lucky for us that we got possession of Nook's Hill. They had placed their cannon so as to fire upon the top of the hill, where they had observed our people marking out the ground; but it was only to elude them; for they began lower upon the hill and nearer the town. It was a very dark, foggy evening, and they had possession of the hill six hours before a gun was fired; and when they did fire, they overshot our people, so that they were covered before morning, and not one man lost, which the enemy no sooner discovered, than Bunker Hill was abandoned, and every man decamped as soon as he could. They found they should not be able to get away if we once got our cannon mounted. Our General may say with Caesar, "*Veni, vidi, et vici.*"

What effect does the expectation of Commissioners have with you? Are they held in disdain as they are here? It is come to that pass now, that the longest sword must decide the contest; and the sword is less dreaded here than the Commissioners.

You mention threats upon B——e. I know of none, nor ever heard of any till you mentioned them. The Tories look a little crestfallen. As for Cleverly, he looks like the knight of the woful countenance. I hear all the mongrel breed are left in Boston, and our people who were prisoners are put in irons and carried off. As to all your own private affairs I generally avoid mentioning them to you; I take the best care I am capable of them. I have found some difficulty attending the only man I have upon the place, being so often taking off. John and Jonathan have taken all the care in his absence, and performed very well. Bass got home very well. My father's horse came home in fine order and much to his satisfaction. Your own very poor.

Cannot you hire a servant where you are? I am sorry you are put to so much difficulty for want of one.

I suppose you do not think one word about coming home, and how you will get home I know not.

I made a mistake in the name of the grammar. It is Tandon's instead of Took's. I wish you could purchase Lord Chesterfield's Letters. I have lately heard them very highly spoken of. I smiled at your couplet of Latin. Your daughter may be able in time to construe it, as she has already made some considerable proficiency in her accidence; but her mamma was obliged to get it translated. Pray write Lord Stirling's character.

I want to know whether you live in any harmony with ——, and how you settled matters. I think he seems in better humor.

I think I do not admire the speech from the rostrum. 'Tis a heavy, inelegant, verbose performance, and did not strike my fancy at all. I am very saucy, I suppose you will say. 'Tis a liberty I take with you. Indulgence is apt to spoil one. Adieu.

P.S. Pray convey me a little paper. I have but enough for one letter more.

Monday Morning

A fine, quiet night. No alarms—no cannon. The more I think of our enemies quitting Boston, the more amazed I am that they should leave such a harbor, such fortifications, such intrenchments, and that we should be in peaceable possession of a town which we expected would cost us a river of blood, without one drop shed. Surely it is the Lord's doings, and it is marvelous in our eyes. Every foot of ground which they obtain now they must fight for, and may they purchase it at a Bunker Hill price.

3. John Adams

Philadelphia, 17 March 1776

OUR WORTHY FRIEND, Frank Dana, arrived here last evening from New York, to which place he came lately from England in the packet. In company with him is a gentleman by the name of Wrixon, who has been a field-officer in the British army, served all the last war in Germany, and has seen service in every part of Europe. He left the army some time ago, and studied law in the Temple, in which science he made a great proficiency. He wrote, lately, a pamphlet under the title of "The Rights of Britons," which he has brought over with him. He is a friend of liberty, and thinks justly of the American question. He has great abilities, as well as experience in the military science, and is an able engineer. I hope we shall employ him.

The Baron de Woedtke we have made a Brigadier-general, and ordered him to Canada. The testimonials in his favor I shall inclose to you. Mr. Dana's account, with which Mr. Wrixon's agrees, ought to extinguish, in every mind, all hopes of reconciliation with Great Britain. This delusive hope has done us great injuries, and, if ever we are ruined, will be the cause of our fall. A hankering after the leeks of Egypt makes us forget the cruelty of her task-masters.

I shall suffer many severe pains on your account for some days. By a vessel from Salem a cannonade was heard from dark till nine o'clock, last night was a week ago. Your vicinity to such scenes of carnage and desolation as, I fear, are now to be seen in Boston and its environs, will throw you into much distress, but I believe in my conscience, I feel more here than you do. The sound of cannon was not so terrible when I was at Braintree as it is here, though I hear it at four hundred miles distance.

You can't imagine what a mortification I sustain in not having received a single line from you since we parted. I suspect some villainy in conveyance. By the relation of Mr. Dana, Mr. Wrixon, and Mr. Temple, Mr. Hutchinson, Mr. Sewall, and their associates are in great disgrace in England. Persons are ashamed to be seen to speak to them. They look despised and sunk.

I shall inclose an extract of a letter from Mons. Dubourg in Paris, and a testimonial in favor of our Prussian General. Adieu.

4. John Adams

Philadelphia, 19 March

YESTERDAY I HAD the long expected and much wished pleasure of a letter from you, of various dates from the 2d to the 10th March. This is the first line I have received since I left you. I wrote you from Watertown, I believe, relating my feast at the Quartermaster-general's with the Caghnawaga Indians, and from Framingham an account of the ordnance there, and from New York I sent you a pamphlet. Hope you received these. Since I arrived here I have written to you as often as I could.

I am much pleased with your caution in your letter, in avoiding names both of persons and places, or any other circumstances which might designate to strangers the writer, or the person written to, or the persons mentioned. Characters and description will do as well.

The lie which you say occasioned such disputes at the tavern was curious enough. Who could make and spread it? I am much obliged to an uncle for his friendship. My worthy fellow-citizens may be easy about me. I never can forsake what I take to be their interests. My own have never been considered by me in competition with theirs. My ease, my domestic happiness, my rural pleasures, my little property, my personal liberty, my reputation, my life, have little weight and ever had in my own estimation, in comparison with the great object of my country. I can say of it with great sincerity, as Horace says of virtue, "To America only and her friends a friend."

You ask what is thought of "Common Sense." Sensible men think there are some whims, some sophisms, some artful addresses to superstitious notions, some keen attempts upon the passions, in this

11

pamphlet. But all agree there is a great deal of good sense delivered in clear, simple, concise, and nervous style. His sentiments of the abilities of America, and of the difficulty of a reconciliation with Great Britain, are generally approved. But his notions and plans of continental government are not much applauded. Indeed, this writer has a better hand in pulling down than building. It has been very generally propagated through the continent that I wrote this pamphlet. But although I could not have written anything in so manly and striking a style, I flatter myself I should have made a more respectable figure as an architect, if I had undertaken such a work. This writer seems to have very inadequate ideas of what is proper and necessary to be done in order to form constitutions for single colonies, as well as a great model of union for the whole.

Your distresses, which you have painted in such lively colors, I feel in every line as I read. I dare not write all that I think upon this occasion. I wish our people had taken possession of Nook's Hill at the same time when they got the other heights, and before the militia was dismissed.

Poor cousin! I pity him. How much soever he may lament certain letters, I don't lament. I never repent of what was no sin. Misfortunes may be borne without whining. But if I can believe Mr. Dana, those letters were much admired in England. I can't help laughing when I write it, because they were really such hasty, crude scraps. If I could have foreseen their fate, they should have been fit to be seen, and worth all the noise they have made. Mr. Dana says they were considered in England as containing a comprehensive idea of what was necessary to be done, and as showing resolution enough to do it. Wretched stuff as they really were, according to him they have contributed somewhat towards making certain persons to be thought the greatest statesmen in the world. So much for vanity.

My love, duty, respects, and compliments wherever they belong. Virginia will be well defended. So will New York. So will South Carolina. America will erelong raise her voice aloud and assume a bolder air.

5. John Adams

Philadelphia, 29 March 1776

I GIVE YOU joy of Boston and Charlestown, once more the habitation of Americans. I am waiting with great impatience for letters from you, which I know will contain many particulars. We are taking precautions to defend every place that is in danger, the Carolinas, Virginia, New York, Canada. I can think of nothing but fortifying Boston harbor. I want more cannon than are to be had. I want a fortification upon Point Alderton, one upon Lovell's Island, one upon George's Island, several upon Long Island, one upon the Moon, one upon Squantum. I want to hear of half a dozen fire-ships, and two or three hundred fire-rafts prepared. I want to hear of row-galleys, floating batteries built, and booms laid across the channel in the narrows, and *Vaisseaux de Frise* sunk in it. I wish to hear that you are translating Braintree commons into the channel. No efforts, no expense are too extravagant for me to wish for, to fortify that harbor so as to make it impregnable. I hope everybody will join and work until it is done.

We have this week lost a very valuable friend of the colonies in Governor Ward, of Rhode Island, by the small-pox in the natural way. He never would hearken to his friends, who have been constantly advising him to be inoculated, ever since the first Congress began. But he would not be persuaded. Numbers, who have been inoculated, have gone through this distemper without any danger, or even confinement, but nothing would do. He must take it in the natural way and die. He was an amiable and a sensible man, a steadfast friend to his country upon very pure principles. His funeral was attended with the same solemnities as Mr. Randolph's. Mr. Stillman being the Anabaptist minister here, of which persuasion was the Governor, was desired by Congress to preach a sermon, which he did with great applause.

Remember me as you ought.

6. Abigail Adams

Braintree, 31 March 1776

I WISH YOU would ever write me a letter half as long as I write you, and tell me, if you may, where your fleet are gone; what sort of defense Virginia can make against our common enemy; whether it is so situated as to make an able defense. Are not the gentry lords, and the common people vassals? Are they not like the uncivilized vassals Britain represents us to be? I hope their riflemen, who have shown themselves very savage and even blood-thirsty, are not a specimen of the generality of the people. I am willing to allow the colony great merit for having produced a Washington; but they have been shamefully duped by a Dunmore.

I have sometimes been ready to think that the passion for liberty cannot be equally strong in the breasts of those who have been accustomed to deprive their fellow-creatures of theirs. Of this I am certain, that it is not founded upon that generous and Christian principle of doing to others as we would that others should do unto us.

Do not you want to see Boston? I am fearful of the small-pox, or I should have been in before this time. I got Mr. Crane to go to our house and see what state it was in. I find it has been occupied by one of the doctors of a regiment; very dirty, but no other damage has been done to it. The few things which were left in it are all gone. Cranch has the key, which he never delivered up. I have wrote to him for it and am determined to get it cleaned as soon as possible and shut it up. I look upon it as a new acquisition of property—a property which one month ago I did not value at a single shilling, and would with pleasure have seen it in flames.

The town in general is left in a better state than we expected; more owing to a precipitate flight than any regard to the inhabitants; though some individuals discovered a sense of honor and justice, and have left the rent of the houses in which they were, for the owners, and the furniture unhurt, or, if damaged, sufficient to make it good. Others have committed abominable ravages. The mansion-house of your President is safe, and the furniture unhurt; while the house and furniture of the Solicitor General have fallen a prey to their own merciless party. Surely the very fiends feel a reverential awe for virtue and patriotism, whilst they detest the parricide and traitor.

I feel very differently at the approach of spring from what I did a month ago. We knew not then whether we could plant or sow with safety, whether where we had tilled we could reap the fruits of our own industry, whether we could rest in our own cottages or whether we should be driven from the seacoast to seek shelter in the wilderness; but now we feel as if we might sit under our own vine and eat the good of the land.

I feel a *gaieté de cœur* to which before I was a stranger. I think the sun looks brighter, the birds sing more melodiously, and Nature puts on a more cheerful countenance. We feel a temporary peace, and the poor fugitives are returning to their deserted habitation.

Though we felicitate ourselves, we sympathize with those who are trembling lest the lot of Boston should be theirs. But they cannot be in similar circumstances unless pusillanimity and cowardice should take possession of them. They have time and warning given them to see the evil and shun it.

I long to hear that you have declared an independency. And, by the way, in the new code of laws which I suppose it will be necessary for you to make, I desire you would remember the ladies and be more generous and favorable to them than your ancestors. Do not put such unlimited power into the hands of the husbands. Remember, all men would be tyrants if they could. If particular care and attention is not paid to the ladies, we are determined to foment a rebellion, and will not hold ourselves bound by any laws in which we have no voice or representation.

That your sex are naturally tyrannical is a truth so thoroughly established as to admit of no dispute; but such of you as wish to be happy willingly give up the harsh title of master for the more tender and endearing one of friend. Why, then, not put it out of the power of the vicious and the lawless to use us with cruelty and indignity with impunity? Men of sense in all ages abhor those customs which treat us only as the vassals of your sex; regard us then as beings placed by Providence under your protection, and in imitation of the Supreme Being make use of that power only for our happiness.

April 5

Not having an opportunity of sending this I shall add a few lines more; though not with a heart so gay. I have been attending the sick chamber of our neighbor Trott whose affliction I most sensibly feel but cannot describe, stripped of two lovely children in one week. George the eldest died on Wednesday and Billy the youngest on Friday, with the canker fever, a terrible disorder so much like the throat distemper that it differs but little from it. Betsy Cranch has been very bad, but upon the recovery. Becky Peck they do not expect will live out the day. Many grown persons are now sick with it, in this street. It rages much in other towns. The mumps too are very frequent. Isaac is now confined with it. Our own little flock are yet well. My heart trembles with anxiety for them. God preserve them.

I want to hear much oftener from you than I do. March 8th was the last date of any that I have yet had. You inquire of me whether I am making saltpetre. I have not yet attempted it, but after soap-making believe I shall make the experiment. I find as much as I can do to manufacture clothing for my family, which would else be naked. I know of but one person in this part of the town who has made any. That is Mr. Tertius Bass, as he is called, who has got very near a hundred-weight which has been found to be very good. I have heard of some others in the other parishes. Mr. Reed, of Weymouth, has been applied to, to go to Andover to the mills which are now at work, and he has gone.

I have lately seen a small manuscript describing the proportions of the various sorts of powder fit for cannon, small arms, and pistols. If it would be of any service your way I will get it transcribed and send it to you. Every one of your friends sends regards, and all the little ones. Your brother's youngest child lies bad with convulsion fits. Adieu. I need not say how much I am your ever faithful friend.

7. Abigail Adams

Braintree, 7 April 1776

I HAVE RECEIVED two letters from you this week. One of the 17th and the other the 19th of March. I know not where one of my letters is gone, unless you have since received it. I certainly wrote you in February, and the first letter I wrote I mention that I had not written before. I have written four letters before this. I believe I have received all yours except one you mention writing from Framingham, which I never heard of before. I have received all the papers you have sent, the oration, and the magazines. In the small papers I sometimes find pieces begun and continued (for instance, Johnstone's speech), but am so unlucky as not to get the papers in order, and miss of seeing the whole.

The removal of the army seems to have stopped the current of news. I want to know to what part of America they are now wandering. It is reported and credited that Manly has taken a schooner belonging to the fleet, richly laden with money, plate, and English goods, with a number of Tories. The particulars I have not yet learned. Yesterday the remains of our worthy General Warren were dug up upon Bunker's Hill, and carried into town, and on Monday are to be interred with all the honors of war.

10 April

The Dr. was buried on Monday; the Masons walking in procession from the State House, with the military in uniforms, and a large concourse of people attending. He was carried into the Chapel, and there a funeral dirge was played, an excellent prayer by Dr. Cooper, and an oration by Mr. Morton, which I hope will be printed. I think the subject must have inspired him. A young fellow could not have wished a finer opportunity to display his talents. The amiable and heroic virtues of the deceased, recent in the minds of the audience; the noble cause to which he fell a martyr; their own sufferings and unparalleled injuries, all fresh in their minds, must have given weight and energy to whatever could be delivered upon the occasion. The dead body, like that of Caesar, before their eyes, whilst each wound,—

> "Like dumb mouths, did ope their ruby lips,
> To beg the voice and utterance of a tongue.
> Woe to the hands that shed this costly blood!
> A curse shall light upon their line.
> Domestic fury, and fierce civil strife
> Shall cumber all the parts of Britton."

11 April

I take my pen and write just as I can get time; my letters will be a strange mixture. I really am "cumbered about many things," and scarcely know which way to turn myself. I miss my partner, and find myself unequal to the cares which fall upon me. I find it necessary to be the directress of our husbandry. Hands are so scarce, that I have not been able to procure one, and add to this that Isaac has been sick with a fever this fortnight, not able to strike a stroke, and a multiplicity of farming business pouring in upon us. In this dilemma I have taken Belcher into pay, and must secure him for the season, as I know not what better course to steer. I hope in time to have the reputation of being as good a *farmeress* as my partner has of being a good statesman. To ask you anything about your return would, I suppose, be asking a question which you cannot answer.

Retirement, rural quiet domestic pleasures, all, all must give place to the weighty cares of state. It would be—

> "Meanly poor in solitude to hide
> An honest zeal, unwarped by party rage."

> "Though certain pains attend the cares of state,
> A good man owes his country to be great,

> Should act abroad the high distinguished part,
> And show, at least, the purpose of his heart."

I hope your Prussian General will answer the high character which is given of him. But we, who have been bred in a land of liberty, scarcely know how to give credit to so unjust and arbitrary a mandate of a despot. To cast off a faithful servant, only for being the unhappy bearer of ill news, degrades the man and dishonors the prince. The Congress, by employing him, have shown a liberality of sentiment not confined to colonies or continents, but, to use the words of "Common Sense," have "carried their friendship on a larger scale, by claiming brotherhood with every European Christian, and may justly triumph in the generosity of the sentiment."

Yesterday, was taken and carried into Cohasset, by three whale-boats, which went from the shore on purpose, a snow from the Grenadas, laden with three hundred and fifty-four puncheons of West India rum, forty-three barrels of sugar, twelve thousand and five hundred-weight of coffee; a valuable prize. A number of Eastern sloops have brought wood into town since the fleet sailed. We have a rumor of Admiral Hopkins being engaged with a number of ships and tenders off Rhode Island, and are anxious to know the event.

Be so good as to send me a list of the vessels which sail with Hopkins, their names, weight of metal, and number of men; all the news you know, etc.

I hear our jurors refuse to serve, because the writs are issued in the King's name. Surely they are for independence.

Write me how you do this winter. I want to say many things I must omit. It is not fit "to wake the soul by tender strokes of art," or to ruminate upon happiness we might enjoy, lest absence become intolerable. Adieu.

Yours.

I wish you would burn all my letters.

8. John Adams

12 April 1776

I INCLOSE A few sheets of paper, and will send more as fast as opportunities present.

Chesterfield's letters are a chequered set. You would not choose to have them in your library. They are like Congreve's plays, stained with libertine morals and base principles.

You will see by the papers the news, the speculations, and the political plans of the day. The ports are opened wide enough at last, and privateers are allowed to prey upon British trade. This is not independency, you know. What is? Why, government in every colony, a confederation among them all, and treaties with foreign nations to acknowledge us a sovereign state, and all that. When these things will be done, or any of them, time must discover. Perhaps the time is near, perhaps a great way off.

21

9. John Adams

YOU JUSTLY COMPLAIN of my short letters, but the critical state of things and the multiplicity of avocations must plead my excuse. You ask where the fleet is? The inclosed papers will inform you. You ask what sort of defense Virginia can make? I believe they will make an able defense. Their militia and minute-men have been some time employed in training themselves, and they have nine battalions of regulars, as they call them, maintained among them, under good officers, at the Continental expense. They have set up a number of manufactories of fire-arms, which are busily employed. They are tolerably supplied with powder, and are successful and assiduous in making saltpetre. Their neighboring sister, or rather daughter colony of North Carolina, which is a warlike colony, and has several battalions at the Continental expense, as well as a pretty good militia, are ready to assist them, and they are in very good spirits and seem determined to make a brave resistance. The gentry are very rich, and the common people very poor. This inequality of property gives an aristocratical turn to all their proceedings, and occasions a strong aversion in their patricians to "Common Sense." But the spirit of these Barons is coming down, and it must submit. It is very true, as you observe, they have been duped by Dunmore. But this is a common case. All the colonies are duped, more or less, at one time and another. A more egregious bubble was never blown up than the story of Commissioners coming to treat with the Congress, yet it has gained credit like a charm, not only with, but against the clearest evidence. I never shall forget the delusion which seized our best and most sagacious friends, the dear inhabitants of Boston, the winter before last. Credulity and the want of foresight are imperfections in the human character, that no politician can sufficiently guard against.

You give me some pleasure by your account of a certain house in Queen Street. I had burned it long ago in imagination. It rises now to my view like a phoenix. What shall I say of the Solicitor General? I pity his pretty children. I pity his father and his sisters. I wish I could be clear that it is no moral evil to pity him and his lady. Upon repentance, they will certainly have a large share in the compassions of many. But let us take warning, and give it to our children. Whenever vanity and gayety, a love of pomp and dress, furniture, equipage, buildings, great company, expensive diversions, and elegant entertainments get the better of the principles and judgments of men or women, there is no knowing where they will stop, nor into what evils, natural, moral, or political, they will lead us.

Your description of your own *gaieté de cœur* charms me. Thanks be to God, you have just cause to rejoice, and may the bright prospect be obscured by no cloud. As to declarations of independency, be patient. Read our privateering laws and our commercial laws. What signifies a word?

As to your extraordinary code of laws, I cannot but laugh. We have been told that our struggle has loosened the bands of government everywhere; that children and apprentices were disobedient; that schools and colleges were grown turbulent; that Indians slighted their guardians, and negroes grew insolent to their masters. But your letter was the first intimation that another tribe, more numerous and powerful than all the rest, were grown discontented. This is rather too coarse a compliment, but you are so saucy, I won't blot it out. Depend upon it, we know better than to repeal our masculine systems. Although they are in full force, you know they are little more than theory. We dare not exert our power in its full latitude. We are obliged to go fair and softly, and, in practice, you know we are the subjects. We have only the name of masters, and rather than give up this, which would completely subject us to the despotism of the petticoat, I hope General Washington and all our brave heroes would fight; I am sure every good politician would plot, as long as he would against despotism, empire, monarchy, aristocracy, oligarchy, or ochlocracy. A fine story, indeed! I begin to think the ministry as deep as they are wicked. After stirring up Tories, land-jobbers, trimmers, bigots, Canadians, Indians, negroes, Hanoverians, Hessians, Russians, Irish Roman Catholics, Scotch renegadoes, at last they have stimulated the ———— to demand new privileges and threaten to rebel.

10. Abigail Adams

Braintree, 14 April 1776

I HAVE MISSED my good friend Colonel Warren from Watertown in the conveyance of my letters. You make no mention of more than one. Write me how many you have had and what the dates were.

I wrote you, upon the 17th of March. Particulars it was not then possible to obtain; and after that, I thought every pen would be employed in writing to you a much more accurate account than I could give you.

The fleet lay in the road almost a fortnight after the town was evacuated. In that time Major Tupper came with a body of men to Germantown, and procured two lighters, and fitted them with every sort of combustible matter, hand grenades, etc., in order to set fire to the fleet. But the very day he was ready, they sailed. And it was said that they had intelligence from Boston of the design. However, he carried the lighters up to town for the next fleet that appears.

Fort Hill is a-fortifying, I suppose, in the best manner. Committees have been appointed to survey the islands, etc., but we are scanty of men. It is said we have not more than two thousand effective men left, and the General thought it necessary to take the heavy cannon with him. We have many pieces spiked up, which they are employed in clearing. About a hundred pieces, I have heard, were left at the castle with their trunnels broken, or spiked. The castle, you have no doubt heard, was burnt by the troops before they sailed, and an attempt was made to blow up the walls, in which, however, they did not succeed any further than to shatter them. There are so many things necessary to be done, that I suppose business moves slowly. At present we all seem to be so happy and so tranquil, that I sometimes think we want another fleet to give some energy and spirit to our motions. But there has been a great overturn that people seem to be hardly recovered from their amazement. Many buildings in town sustained great damages, more particularly at the south end. The furniture of many houses was carried off or broken in pieces. Dr. Gardiner left all his furniture and medicine, valued, it is said, at four hundred sterling. Dr. Lloyd is still in town; Dr. Whitworth too. Both ought to be transported. Mr. Goldthwait is in town. All the records of which he had the care safe, though it seems part of them were carried into Boston. All the papers relating to the Probate Courts are missing. Mr. Lovell, and all the prisoners taken at the Charlestown battle, are carried off. The bells are all in town; never were taken down. The officers and Tories have lived a life of dissipation. Inclosed is a prologue of Burgoyne's, with a parody written in Boston, soon after it was acted. Burgoyne is a better poet than soldier.

As to goods of any kind, we cannot tell what quantity there is. Only two or three shops open. Goods at most extravagant prices. All the better to promote manufactures. The small-pox prevents my going to town; several have broke out with it in the army since they went into Boston. I cannot help wishing that it would spread. I think the country is in more danger than ever. I am anxious about it. If it should spread there is but one thing would prevent my going down to our own house and having it with all our children, and I don't know but I should be tempted to run you in debt for it. There is talk of raising another regiment. If they should, I fear we shall suffer in our husbandry. Labor is very high. I cannot hire a man for six months under twenty pounds lawful money. The works upon the Neck are leveling. We keep guards upon the shores yet. Manly has taken a vessel-load of Tories. Among them is Black, the Scotchman, and Brazen-head Jackson, Hill, the baker, etc. What can be done with them? I think they ought to be transported to England. I would advertise for Tory transports.

Hanover has made large quantities of saltpetre. This week we are to hold court here, but I do not imagine anything will be done. I have a letter from you the 29th of March. It is said there is one from Mr. Gerry the 3d of April, acquainting us with your opening trade. Who is the writer of "Common Sense"? of "Cato"? of "Cassandra"? I wish you would, according to promise, write me an account of Lord Stirling. We know nothing about him here.

All the Tories look crest-fallen. Several deserters from on board the commodore's ship say that it is very sickly on board. We have only that and two or three cutters besides. We fear that a brig, laden with seventy tons of powder, which sailed from Newburyport, has fallen into the enemy's hands upon her return.

I rejoice in the Southern victories. The oration was a very elegant performance, but not without much art,—a few strokes which to me injure it. I know not anything further which I ought to say but that I am most affectionately yours.

11. John Adams

15 April

I SEND YOU every newspaper that comes out, and I send you, now and then, a few sheets of paper, but this article is as scarce here as with you. I would send a quire, if I could get a conveyance.

I write you now and then a line, as often as I can, but I can tell you no news but what I send in the public papers.

We are waiting, it is said, for Commissioners; a messiah that will never come. This story of Commissioners is as arrant an illusion as ever was hatched in the brain of an enthusiast, a politician, or a maniac. I have laughed at it, scolded at it, grieved at it, and I don't know but I may, at an unguarded moment, have rip'd at it. But it is vain to reason against such delusions. I was very sorry to see, in a letter from the General, that he had been bubbled with it; and still more, to see, in a letter from my sagacious friend W., at Plymouth, that he was taken in too.

My opinion is that the Commissioners and the commission have been here (I mean in America), these two months. The Governors, Mandamus Councillors, Collectors and Comptrollers, and Commanders of the army and navy, I conjecture, compose the list, and their power is to receive submissions. But we are not in a very submissive mood. They will get no advantage of us. We shall go on to perfection, I believe. I have been very busy for some time; have written about ten sheets of paper with my own hand, about some trifling affairs, which I may mention some time or other—not now, for fear of accidents.

What will come of this labor, time will discover. I shall get nothing by it, I believe, because I never get anything by anything that I do. I am sure the public or posterity ought to get something. I believe my children will think I might as well have thought and labored a little, night and day, for their benefit. But I will not bear the reproaches of my children. I will tell them that I studied and labored to procure a free constitution of government for them to solace themselves under, and if they do not prefer this to ample fortune, to ease and elegance, they are not my children, and I care not what becomes of them. They shall live upon thin diet, wear mean clothes, and work hard with cheerful hearts and free spirits, or they may be the children of the earth, or of no one, for me.

John has genius, and so has Charles. Take care that they don't go astray. Cultivate their minds, inspire their little hearts, raise their wishes. Fix their attention upon great and glorious objects. Root out every little thing. Weed out every meanness. Make them great and manly. Teach them to scorn injustice, ingratitude, cowardice, and falsehood. Let them revere nothing but religion, morality, and liberty.

Nabby and Tommy are not forgotten by me, although I did not mention them before. The first, by reason of her sex, requires a different education from the two I have mentioned. Of this, you are the only judge. I want to send each of my little pretty flock some present or other. I have walked over this city twenty times, and gaped at every shop, like a countryman, to find something, but could not. Ask every one of them what they would choose to have, and write it to me in your next letter. From this I shall judge of their taste and fancy and discretion.

12. John Adams to John Q. Adams

Philadelphia, 18 April 1776

I THANK YOU for your agreeable letter of the 24th of March. I rejoice with you that our friends are once more in possession of the town of Boston; am glad to hear that so little damage is done to our house.

I hope you and your sister and brothers will take proper notice of these great events, and remember under whose wise and kind Providence they are all conducted. Not a sparrow falls, nor a hair is lost, but by the direction of infinite wisdom. Much less are cities conquered and evacuated. I hope that you will all remember how many losses, dangers, and inconveniences have been borne by your parents, and the inhabitants of Boston in general, for the sake of preserving freedom for you and yours, and I hope you will all follow the virtuous example, if, in any future time, your country's liberties shall be in danger, and suffer every human evil rather than give them up. My love to your mamma, your sister and brothers, and all the family. I am your affectionate father.

13. Abigail Adams

18 April 1776

I CANNOT OMIT so good an opportunity as offers by Mr. Church of telling you that we are all well. I wrote you two letters last week, which I sent to Watertown. In those I said everything that occurred to my mind. Nothing since of any importance has taken place. The 19th of April, ever memorable for America as the Ides of March to Rome and to Caesar, is fixed upon for the examination of the Tories by a committee from the General Court. I could have wished that some other persons in the room of one or two might have been chosen. It is so dangerous mentioning names that I refer you to Mr. Church for the names of the committee, and then you will easily guess who I mean.

I wish I could tell you that business in the fortification way went on briskly; but a western member of the General Court, who has great influence there, has got it into his head that Fort Hill and Noddle's Island are sufficient, and though a man possessed of a very good heart, is sometimes obstinately wrong.

The Court of Sessions sat yesterday, and went on with business very smoothly.

We hear that Congress has declared a free trade; and I give you joy of the success of Admiral Hopkins, not only in his expedition, but in his success upon his return. Great Britain, I think, is not quite omnipotent at sea any more than upon the land.

You promised to come and see me in May or June. Shall I expect you, or do you determine to stay out the year? I very well remember when the eastern circuits of the courts, which lasted a month, were thought an age, and an absence of three months intolerable. But we are carried from step to step, and from one degree to another, to endure that which at first we think impossible.

But I assure you I am obliged to make use of reason and philosophy in addition to custom, to feel patient. Be assured I always remember you as I ought, that is, with the kindest affection.

PORTIA

14. Abigail Adams

21 April 1776

I HAVE TO acknowledge the receipt of a very few lines dated the 12th of April. You make no mention of the whole sheets I have wrote to you, by which I judge you either never received them, or that they were so lengthy as to be troublesome; and in return you have set me an example of being very concise. I believe I shall not take the hint, but give as I love to receive. Mr. Church talked a week ago of setting off for Philadelphia. I wrote by him, but suppose it has not yet gone. You have perhaps heard that the bench is filled by Messrs. Foster and Sullivan, so that a certain person is now excluded. I own I am not of so forgiving a disposition as to wish to see him holding a place which he refused merely from a spirit of envy.

I give up my request for Chesterfield's "Letters," submitting entirely to your judgment, as I have ever found you ready to oblige me in this way whenever you thought it would contribute either to my entertainment or improvement. I was led to the request from reading the following character of him in my favorite Thomson, from some spirited and patriotic speeches of his in the reign of George II:—

> "O thou whose wisdom, solid yet refined,
>   Whose patriot-virtues and consummate skill
>   To touch the finer springs that move the world,
>   Joined to whate'er the Graces can bestow,
>   And all Apollo's animating fire,
>   Give thee with pleasing dignity to shine
>   At once the guardian, ornament, and joy
>   Of polished life. Permit the rural muse,

> O Chesterfield! to grace thee with her song,
> Ere to the shades again she humbly flies;
> Indulge her fond ambition, in thy train
> (For every muse has in thy train a place)
> To mark thy various, full accomplished mind,—
> To mark that spirit which, with British scorn,
> Rejects th' allurements of corrupted power;
> That elegant politeness which excels,
> Even in the judgment of presumptuous France,
> The boasted manner of her shining court;
> That wit, the vivid energy of sense,
> The truth of nature, which, with Attic point,
> And kind, well-tempered satire, smoothly keen,
> Steals through the soul, and, without pain, corrects."

I think the speculations you inclose prove that there is full liberty of the press. Cato shows he has a bad cause to defend; whilst the Forester writes with a spirit peculiar to himself, and leads me to think that he has an intimate acquaintance with "Common Sense."

We have intelligence of the arrival of some of the Tory fleet at Halifax; that they are much distressed for want of houses,—obliged to give six dollars per month for one room; provisions scarce and dear. Some of them with six or eight children around them, sitting upon the rocks, crying, not knowing where to lay their heads.

Just Heaven has given them to taste of the same cup of affliction which they one year ago administered with such callous hearts to thousands of their fellow-citizens; but with this difference, that they fly from the injured and enraged country, whilst pity and commiseration received the sufferers whom they inhumanly drove from their dwellings.

I would fain hope that the time may not be far distant when those things you hint at may be carried into execution.

> "Oh! are ye not those patriots in whose power
> That best, that godlike luxury is placed
> Of blessing thousands, thousands yet unborn
> Thro' late posterity? Ye large of soul,
> Cheer up dejected industry, and give
> A double harvest to the pining swain.
> Teach thou, the laboring hand the sweets of toil

How, by the finest art, the native robe
To weave; how, white as Hyperborean snow,
To form the lucid lawn; with venturous oar
How to dash wide the billow; nor look on,
Shamefully passive, while Britannia's fleets
Defraud us of the glittering finny swarms
That heave our friths and swarm upon our shores
How all-enlivening trade to rouse, and wing
The prosperous sail from every growing port
Uninjured round the sea-encircled globe."

It is rumored here that Admiral Hopkins is blocked up in Newport harbor by a number of men-of-war. If so, 'tis a very unlucky circumstance. As to fortifications, those who preside in the Assembly can give you a much better account than I.

I heard yesterday that a number of gentlemen who were together at Cambridge thought it highly proper that a committee of ladies should be chosen to examine the Tory ladies, and proceeded to the choice of three—Mrs. Winthrop, Mrs. Warren, and your humble servant.

I could go on and give you a long list of domestic affairs, but they would only serve to embarrass you and noways relieve me. I hope it will not be long before things will be brought into such a train as that you may be spared to your family.

Your brother has lost his youngest child with convulsion fits. Your mother is well and always desires to be remembered to you. Nabby is sick with the mumps,—a very disagreeable disorder. You have not once told me how you do. I judge you are well, as you seem to be in good spirits. I bid you good night. All the little flock send duty, and want to see p———a.

Adieu. Shall I say, remember me as you ought?

15. John Adams

Philadelphia, 23 April 1776

THIS IS ST. GEORGE'S day, a festival celebrated by the English, as St. Patrick's is by the Irish, St. David's by the Welsh, and St. Andrew's by the Scotch. The natives of Old England in this city heretofore formed a society, which they called St. George's Club or St. George's Society. Upon the 23d of April, annually, they had a great feast. But the Tories and politics have made a schism in the society, so that one part of them are to meet and dine at the City Tavern, and the other at the Bunch of Grapes, Israel Jacobs's, and a third party go out of town. One set are stanch Americans, another stanch Britons, and a third, half-way men, neutral beings, moderate men, prudent folks; for such is the division among men upon all occasions and every question. This is the account which I have from my barber, who is one of the society, and zealous on the side of America, and one of the Philadelphia Associators.

This curious character of a barber I have a great inclination to draw, for your amusement. He is a little, dapper fellow, short and small, but active and lively. A tongue as fluent and voluble as you please, wit at will, and a memory or an invention which never leaves him at a loss for a story to tell you for your entertainment. He has seen great company. He has dressed hair and shaved faces at Bath, and at Court. He is acquainted with several of the nobility and gentry, particularly Sir William Meredith. He married a girl, the daughter of a Quaker in this place, of whom he tells many droll stories. He is a serjeant in one of the companies of some battalion or other here. He frequents, of evenings, a beer house kept by one Weaver, in the city, where he has many curious disputes and adventures, and meets many odd characters.

I believe you will think me very idle to write you so trifling a letter, upon so uninteresting a subject, at a time when my country is fighting *pro aris et focis*. But I assure you I am glad to chat with this barber, while he is shaving and combing me, to divert myself from less agreeable thoughts. He is so sprightly and good-humored that he contributes, more than I could have imagined, to my comfort in this life. Burne has prepared a string of toasts for the club to drink to-day at Israel's.

The thirteen united colonies.

The free and independent States of America.

The Congress for the time being.

The American army and navy.

The Governor and Council of South Carolina, etc., etc., etc.

A happy election for the Whigs on the first of May, etc.

16. John Adams

Philadelphia, 28 April 1776

YESTERDAY I RECEIVED two letters from you from the 7th to the 14th of April. I have received all your letters, and I am not certain I wrote one from Framingham. The one I mean contains an account of my dining with the Indians at Mr. Mifflin's. It gives me concern to think of the many cares you must have upon your mind. Am glad that you have taken [Belcher] into play, and that Isaac is well before now, I hope. Your reputation as a farmer, or anything else you undertake, I dare answer for. Your partner's character as a statesman is much more problematical.

As to my return, I have not a thought of it. Journeys of such a length are tedious, and expensive both of time and money, neither of which is my own. I hope to spend the next Christmas where I did the last, and after that I hope to be relieved; for by that time, I shall have taken a pretty good trick at helm, whether the vessel has been well steered or not. But if my countrymen should insist upon my serving them another year, they must let me bring my whole family with me. Indeed, I could keep house here, with my partner, four children, and two servants, as cheap as I maintain myself here with two horses and a servant at lodgings.

Instead of domestic felicity, I am destined to public contentions. Instead of rural felicity, I must reconcile myself to the smoke and noise of a city. In the place of private peace, I must be distracted with the vexation of developing the deep intrigues of politicians, and must assist in conducting the arduous operations of war, and think myself well rewarded if my private pleasure and interests are sacrificed, as they ever have been and will be, to the happiness of others.

You tell me our jurors refuse to serve, because the writs are issued in the King's name. I am very glad to hear that they discover so much sense and spirit. I learn, from another letter, that the General Court have left out of their bills the year of his reign, and that they are making a law that the same name shall be left out of all writs, commissions, and all law processes. This is good news too. The same will be the case in all the colonies, very soon.

You ask me, how I have done, the winter past. I have not enjoyed so good health as last fall. But I have done complaining of anything. Of ill-health I have no right to complain, because it is given me by Heaven. Of meanness, of envy, of littleness, of ——, of ——, of ——, I have reason and right to complain, but I have too much contempt to use that right. There is such a mixture of folly, littleness, and knavery in this world, that I am weary of it, and although I behold it with unutterable contempt and indignation, yet the public good requires that I should take no notice of it by word or by letter. And to this public good I will conform.

You will see an account of the fleet in some of the papers I have sent you. I give you joy of the Admiral's success. I have vanity enough to take to myself a share in the merit of the American navy. It was always a measure that my heart was much engaged in, and I pursued it for a long time against the wind and tide, but at last obtained it.

Is there no way for two friendly souls to converse together although the bodies are four hundred miles off? Yes, by letter. But I want a better communication. I want to hear you think or to see your thoughts. The conclusion of your letter makes my heart throb more than a cannonade would. You bid me burn your letters. But I must forget you first. In yours of April 14 you say you miss our friend in the conveyance of your letters. Don't hesitate to write by the post. Seal well. Don't miss a single post. You take it for granted that I have particular intelligence of everything from others, but I have not. If any one wants a vote for a commission he vouchsafes me a letter, but tells me very little news. I have more particulars from you than any one else. Pray keep me constantly informed what ships are in the harbor and what fortifications are going on. I am quite impatient to hear of more vigorous measures for fortifying Boston harbor. Not a moment should be neglected. Every man ought to go down, as they did after the battle of Lexington, and work until it is done. I would willingly pay half a dozen hands myself, and subsist them, rather than it should not be done immediately. It is of more importance than to raise corn. You say "inclosed is a prologue and a parody," but neither was inclosed. If you did not forget it, the letter has been opened, and the inclosures taken out. If the small-pox spreads, run me in debt. I received, a post or two past, a letter from your uncle at Salem, containing a most friendly and obliging invitation to you and yours to go and have the distemper at his house if it should spread. He has one or two in his family to have it.

The writer of "Common Sense" and "The Forester" is the same person. His name is Paine, a gentleman about two years ago from England, a man who, General Lee says, has genius in his eyes. The writer of "Cassandra" is said to be Mr. James Cannon, a tutor in the Philadelphia College. "Cato" is reported here to be Doctor Smith—a match for Brattle. The oration was an insolent performance. A motion was made to thank the orator, and ask a copy, but opposed with great spirit and vivacity from every part of the room, and at last withdrawn, lest it should be rejected, as it certainly would have been, with indignation. The orator then printed it himself, after leaving out or altering some offensive passages. This is one of the many irregular and extravagant characters of the age. I never heard one single person speak well of anything about him but his abilities, which are generally allowed to be good. The appointment of him to make the oration was a great oversight and mistake.

The late act of Parliament has made so deep an impression upon people's minds throughout the colonies, it is looked upon as the last stretch of oppression, that we are hastening rapidly to great events. Governments will be up everywhere before midsummer, and an end to royal style, titles, and authority. Such mighty revolutions make a deep impression on the minds of men, and set many violent passions at work. Hope, fear, joy, sorrow, love, hatred, malice, envy, revenge, jealousy, ambition, avarice, resentment, gratitude, and every other passion, feeling, sentiment, principle, and imagination were never in more lively exercise than they are now from Florida to Canada inclusively. May God in his providence overrule the whole for the good of mankind. It requires more serenity of temper, a deeper understanding, and more courage than fell to the lot of Marlborough to ride in this whirlwind.

17. Abigail Adams

Braintree, 7 May 1776

HOW MANY ARE the solitary hours I spend ruminating upon the past and anticipating the future, whilst you, overwhelmed with the cares of state, have but a few moments you can devote to any individual. All domestic pleasures and enjoyments are absorbed in the great and important duty you owe your country, "for our country is, as it were, a secondary god, and the first and greatest parent. It is to be preferred to parents, wives, children, friends, and all things,—the gods only excepted; for, if our country perishes, it is as impossible to save an individual as to preserve one of the fingers of a mortified hand." Thus do I suppress every wish, and silence every murmur, acquiescing in a painful separation from the companion of my youth and the friend of my heart.

I believe 'tis near ten days since I wrote you a line. I have not felt in a humor to entertain you. If I had taken up my pen perhaps some unbecoming invective might have fallen from it. The eyes of our rulers have been closed, and a lethargy has seized almost every member. I fear a fatal security has taken possession of them. Whilst the building is on flame, they tremble at the expense of water to quench it. In short, two months have elapsed since the evacuation of Boston, and very little has been done in that time to secure it, or the harbor, from future invasion. The people are all in a flame, and no one among us, that I have heard of, even mentions expense. They think, universally, that there has been an amazing neglect somewhere. Many have turned out as volunteers to work upon Noddle's Island, and many more would go upon Nantasket, if it was once set on foot. "'Tis a maxim of state, that power and liberty are like heat and moisture. Where they are well mixed, everything prospers; where they are single, they are destructive."

A government of more stability is much wanted in this colony, and they are ready to receive it from the hands of the Congress. And since I have begun with maxims of state, I will add another, namely, that a people may let a king fall, yet still remain a people; but, if a king let his people slip from him, he is no longer a king. And as this is most certainly our case, why not proclaim to the world, in decisive terms, your own importance?

Shall we not be despised by foreign powers, for hesitating so long at a word?

I cannot say that I think you are very generous to the ladies; for, whilst you are proclaiming peace and good-will to men, emancipating all nations, you insist upon retaining an absolute power over wives. But you must remember that arbitrary power is like most other things which are very hard, very liable to be broken; and, notwithstanding all your wise laws and maxims, we have it in our power, not only to free ourselves, but to subdue our masters, and, without violence, throw both your natural and legal authority at our feet;—

> "Charm by accepting, by submitting sway,
> Yet have our humor most when we obey."

I thank you for several letters which I have received since I wrote last; they alleviate a tedious absence, and I long earnestly for a Saturday evening, and experience a similar pleasure to that which I used to find in the return of my friend upon that day after a week's absence. The idea of a year dissolves all my philosophy.

Our little ones, whom you so often recommend to my care and instruction, shall not be deficient in virtue or probity, if the precepts of a mother have their desired effect; but they would be doubly enforced, could they be indulged with the example of a father alternately before them. I often point them to their sire,—

> "engaged in a corrupted state,
> Wrestling with vice and faction."

9 May

I designed to have finished the sheet, but, an opportunity offering, I close, only just informing you that, May the 7th, our privateers took two prizes in the bay, in fair sight of the man-of-war; one, a brig from Ireland; the other from Fayal, loaded with wine, brandy, etc.; the other with beef, etc. The wind was east, and a flood tide, so that the tenders could not get out, though they tried several times; the lighthouse fired signal guns, but all would not do. They took them in triumph, and carried them into Lynn. Johnny and Charles have the mumps, a bad disorder, but they are not very bad. Pray be kind enough to remember me at all times, and write, as often as you possibly can, to your

PORTIA

18. Abigail Adams

9 May 1776

I THIS DAY received yours of the 20th of April, accompanied with a letter upon government. Upon reading it I somehow or other felt an uncommon affection for it. I could not help thinking it was a near relation of a very intimate friend of mine. If I am mistaken in its descent, I know it has a near affinity to the sentiments of that person. And though I cannot pretend to be an adept in the art of government, yet it looks rational that a government of good laws well administered should carry with them the fairest prospect of happiness to a community, as well as to individuals. But as this is a prerogative to which your sex lay an almost exclusive claim, I shall quit the subject after having quoted a passage in favor of a republic, from an anonymous author entitled "Essays on the Genius and Writings of Pope."

"The fine arts in short, are naturally attendant upon power and luxury. But the sciences require unlimited freedom to raise them to their full vigor and growth. In a monarchy there may be poets, painters, and musicians, but orators, historians, and philosophers can exist in a republic alone. The Roman nation, by their unjust attempt upon the liberty of the world, justly lost their own, and with their liberty they lost not only their force of eloquence, but even their style and language itself."

This province is not in the most agreeable situation at present. It wants a poise, a stability, which it does not possess. The Council have recommended it to the Superior Court to sit at Ipswich next term. Judge Cushing called upon me yesterday with his lady, and made me a very friendly visit; said he wished earnestly for the presence

43

of the Chief Justice. He had many things he wished to say to him. I requested him to write, and he has promised to.

The spirit of fortification has just waked, and we are now pursuing with vigor what ought before this time to have been completed. Fort Hill, the Castle, Dorchester Points, Noddle's Island are almost completed. A committee are sent down to Nantasket, and orders are given to fortify the Moon, George's Island, etc. I believe Noddle's Island has been done by subscription. Six hundred inhabitants of the town meet every morning in the town house, from whence they march with fife and drum, with Mr. Gordon, Mr. Skilman, and Mr. Lothrop at their head, to the Long Wharf, where they embark for the island; and it comes to the subscribers' turn to work two days in a week.

You have no doubt heard of the appointment of your friend as judge. He seems loath to accept, and his lady I think loath that he should. Surely it does not look well to have those offices bandied about from hand to hand; if they could not obtain one from the bar, that gentleman will fill the place with honor to himself and his brethren. But Mr. Lowell ought to have come in, instead of some others; but there are some in Council who require more than Heaven: that demands only repentance and amendment.

Let me hear from you often.   Yours unfeignedly.

19. John Adams

Philadelphia, 12 May 1776

YOURS OF 21 APRIL came to hand yesterday. I send you regularly every newspaper, and write as often as I can; but I feel more skittish about writing than I did, because, since the removal of headquarters' to New York, we have no express, and very few individual travellers; and the post I am not quite confident in; however, I shall write as I can.

What shall I do with my office? I want to resign it for a thousand reasons. Would you advise me?

There has been a gallant battle in Delaware River between the galleys and two men-of-war, the *Roebuck* and *Liverpool,* in which the men-of-war came off second best; which has diminished, in the minds of the people on both sides of the river, the terror of a man-of-war.

I long to hear a little of my private affairs; yet I dread it, too, because I know you must be perplexed and distressed. I wish it was in my power to relieve you. It gives me great pleasure to learn that our rulers are, at last, doing something towards the fortification of Boston. But I am inexpressibly chagrined to find that the enemy is fortifying on George's Island. I never shall be easy until they are completely driven out of that harbor, and effectually prevented from ever getting in again. As you are a politician and now elected into an important office, that of judgess of the Tory ladies, which will give you, naturally, an influence with your sex, I hope you will be instant, in season and out of season, in exhorting them to use their influence with the gentlemen, to fortify upon George's Island, Lovell's, Pettick's, Long, or wherever else it is proper. Send down fire ships and rafts, and burn to ashes those pirates. I am out of patience with the languid, lethargic councils of the province, at such a critical, important moment, puzzling their heads about twopenny fees, and confession bills, and what not, when the harbor of Boston is defenseless. If I was there, I should storm and thunder like Demosthenese or scold like a tooth-drawer. Do ask Mr. Wibird and Mr. Weld and Mr. Taft to preach about it. I am ashamed, vexed, angry to the last degree. Our people, by their torpitude, have invited the enemy to come to Boston again, and I fear they will have the civility and politeness to accept the invitation.

Your uncle has never answered my letter. Thank the Dr.; he has written me a most charming letter, full of intelligence and very sensible and useful remarks. I will pay the debt, as far as my circumstances will admit, and as soon. But I hope my friends will not wait for regular returns from me. I have not yet left off pitying "the fifty or sixty men"; and if my friends knew all that I do, they would pity too. Betsey Smith, lazy hussy, has not written me a line, a great while. I wish she was married—then she would have some excuse. Duty to Pa. Love to all. How is the family over against the church?

20. John Adams

17 May 1776

I HAVE THIS morning heard Mr. Duffield, upon the signs of the times. He ran a parallel between the case of Israel and that of America; and between the conduct of Pharaoh and that of George. Jealousy that the Israelites would throw off the government of Egypt made him issue his edict that the midwives should cast the children into the river, and the other edict, that the men should make a large revenue of bricks without straw. He concluded, that the course of events indicated strongly the design of Providence that we should be separated from Great Britain, etc.

Is it not a saying of Moses, "Who am I, that I should go in and out before this great people"? When I consider the great events which are passed, and those greater which are rapidly advancing, and that I may have been instrumental in touching some springs and turning some small wheels, which have had and will have such effects, I feel an awe upon my mind which is not easily described. Great Britain has at last driven America to the last step, a complete separation from her; a total, absolute independence, not only of her Parliament, but of her crown, for such is the amount of the resolve of the 15th. Confederation among ourselves, or alliances with foreign nations, are not necessary to a perfect separation from Britain. That is effected by extinguishing all authority under the crown, Parliament, and nation, as the resolution for instituting governments has done, to all intents and purposes. Confederation will be necessary for our internal concord, and alliances may be so for our external defense.

I have reasons to believe that no colony, which shall assume a government under the people, will give it up. There is something very unnatural and odious in a government a thousand leagues off. A whole government of our own choice, managed by persons whom we love, revere, and can confide in, has charms in it for which men will fight. Two young gentlemen from South Carolina in this city, who were in Charlestown when their new constitution was promulgated, and when their new Governor and Council and Assembly walked out in procession, attended by the guards, company of cadets, light horse, etc., told me that they were beheld by the people with transports and tears of joy. The people gazed at them with a kind of rapture. They both told me that the reflection that these were gentlemen whom they all loved, esteemed, and revered, gentlemen of their own choice, whom they could trust, and whom they could displace, if any of them should behave amiss, affected them so that they could not help crying. They say their people will never give up this government. One of these gentlemen is a relation of yours, a Mr. Smith, son of Mr. Thomas Smith. I shall give him this letter or another to you.

A privateer fitted out here by Colonel Roberdeau and Major Bayard since our resolves for privateering, I am this moment informed, has taken a valuable prize. This is encouragement at the beginning.

In one or two of your letters, you remind me to think of you as I ought. Be assured, there is not an hour of the day in which I don't think of you as I ought, that is, with every sentiment of tenderness, esteem, and admiration.

21. John Adams

Philadelphia, 22 May 1776

WHEN A MAN is seated in the midst of forty people, some of whom are talking, and others whispering, it is not easy to think what is proper to write. I shall send you the newspapers, which will inform you of public affairs, and the particular flickerings of parties in this colony. I am happy to learn from your letter that a flame is at last raised among the people, for the fortification of the harbor. Whether Nantasket or Point Alderton would be proper posts to be taken, I can't say. But I would fortify every place which is proper, and which cannon could be obtained for. Generals Gates and Mifflin are now here. General Washington will be here to-morrow, when we shall consult and deliberate concerning the operations of the ensuing campaign.

We have dismal accounts from Europe of the preparations against us. This summer will be very important to us. We shall have a severe trial of our patience, fortitude, and perseverance. But I hope we shall do valiantly, and tread down our enemies.

I have some thoughts of petitioning the General Court for leave to bring my family here. I am a lonely, forlorn creature here. It used to be some comfort to me that I had a servant and some horses. They composed a sort of family for me. But now, there is not one creature here that I seem to have any kind of relation to. It is a cruel reflection, which very often comes across me, that I should be separated so far from those babes whose education and welfare lie so near my heart. But greater misfortunes than these must not divert us from superior duties.

Your sentiments of the duties we owe to our country are such as become the best of women and the best of men. Among all the disappointments and perplexities which have fallen to my share in life, nothing has contributed so much to support my mind as the choice blessing of a wife whose capacity enabled her to comprehend, and whose pure virtue obliged her to approve, the views of her husband. This has been the cheering consolation of my heart in my most solitary, gloomy, and disconsolate hours. In this remote situation, I am deprived in a great measure of this comfort. Yet I read and read again your charming letters, and they serve me, in some faint degree, as a substitute for the company and conversation of the writer. I want to take a walk with you in the garden, to go over to the common, the plain, the meadow. I want to take Charles in one hand and Tom in the other, and walk with you, Nabby on your right hand and John upon my left, to view the corn fields, the orchards, etc.

Alas, poor imagination! how faintly and imperfectly do you supply the want of originality and reality. But instead of these pleasing scenes of domestic life, I hope you will not be disturbed with the alarms of war. I hope, yet I fear.

22. John Adams

Philadelphia, 27 May 1776

I HAVE THREE of your favors before me, one of May 7, another of May 9, and a third of May 14th. The last has given me relief from many anxieties. It relates wholly to private affairs, and contains such an account of wise and prudent management as makes me very happy. I begin to be jealous that our neighbors will think affairs more discreetly conducted in my absence than at any other time. Whether your suspicions concerning a letter under a marble cover are just or not, it is best to say little about it. It is a hasty, hurried thing, and of no great consequence, calculated for a meridian at a great distance from New England. If it has done no good, it will do no harm. It has contributed to set people thinking upon the subject, and in this respect has answered its end. The manufacture of governments having, since the publication of that letter, been as much talked of as that of saltpetre was before.

I rejoice at your account of the spirit of fortification, and the good effects of it. I hope by this time you are in a tolerable posture of defense. The inhabitants of Boston have done themselves great honor by their laudable zeal, the worthy clergymen, especially.

I think you shine as a stateswoman of late, as well as a farmeress. Pray where do you get your maxims of state? They are very apropos. I am much obliged to Judge Cushing and his lady for their polite visit to you. I should be very happy to see him, and converse with him about many things, but cannot hope for that pleasure very soon. The affairs of America are in so critical a state, such great events are struggling into birth, that I must not quit this station at this time. Yet I dread the melting heats of a Philadelphia summer,

51

and know not how my frail constitution will endure it. Such constant care, such incessant application of mind, drinking up and exhausting the finer spirits, upon which life and health so essentially depend, will wear away a stronger man than I am. Yet I will not shrink from this danger or this toil. While my health shall be such that I can discharge, in any tolerable manner, the duties of this important post, I will not desert it.

I am pleased to hear that the Superior Court is to sit at Ipswich in June. This will contribute to give stability to the government, I hope, in all its branches. But I presume other steps will be taken for this purpose. A Governor and Lieutenant-governor, I hope, will be chosen, and the Constitution a little more fixed. I hope too, that the Council will, this year, be more full, and augmented by the addition of good men. I hope Mr. Bowdoin will be Governor, if his health will permit, and Dr. Winthrop Lieutenant-governor. These are wise, learned, and prudent men. The first has a great fortune and wealthy connections. The other has the advantage of a name and family which is much reverenced, besides his personal abilities and virtues, which are very great.

Our friend, I sincerely hope, will not refuse his appointment. For although I have ever thought that the bench should be filled from the bar, and once labored successfully to effect it, yet as the gentlemen have seen fit to decline, I know of no one who would do more honor to the station than my friend. None would be so agreeable to me, whether I am to sit by him or before him. I suppose it must be disagreeable to him and his lady, because he loves to be upon his farm, and they both love to be together. But you must tell them of a couple of their friends, who are as fond of living together, who are obliged to sacrifice their rural amusements and domestic happiness to the requisitions of the public.

The Generals, Washington, Gates, and Mifflin, are all here, and we shall derive spirit, unanimity, and vigor from their presence and advice. I hope you will have some general officers at Boston soon. I am, with constant wishes and prayers for your health and prosperity, forever yours.

23. Abigail Adams

WHAT CAN BE the reason I have not heard from you since the 20th of April, and now 'tis the 27th of May. My anxious, foreboding heart fears every evil, and my nightly slumbers are tortured. I have sent and sent again to the post-office, which is now kept in Boston at the office of the former Solicitor General. Not one line for me, though your handwriting is to be seen to several others. Not a scrip have I had since the General Assembly rose, and our worthy friend W———n left Watertown. I fear you are sick. The very idea casts such a gloom upon my spirits that I cannot recover them for hours, nor reason myself out of my fears. Surely if letters are delivered to any other hand than those to whose care they are directed, 'tis cruel to detain them. I believe for the future you had better direct them to be left in the post-office, from whence I shall be sure of obtaining them.

I am desired by sister A———s to ask you if you will take twenty-eight acres of woodland which she mentioned to you. It must be sold, has a very fine growth of walnut wood upon it, as well as other wood, 'tis prized at forty shillings per acre, which by looking into his deed of it, I find to be the same he gave for it. The distance which it lies from us is the chief objection in my mind. You will be so good as to send me word as soon as you receive this. They are about settling the estate as soon as possible. What can be done with or about the lighter I know not. I was told that she was taken for a fire ship, but was misinformed. There is no regular account of anything but the ropes, cable, and sails, nor anything which appears to show the cost of her. I think it can only be left to those who built about that time to say what they believe she cost. They have prized on half of her very low £33.8.4. I have asked my uncle Q———y to assist in your stead. The watch, she says, you desired to have. I know nothing about it; not having heard you mention it. She sets it at six pounds.

I wrote you two letters about a fortnight ago which were both covered together. Hope you have received them. We have no news here but what you will be informed of long before this reaches you, unless it is the politics of the town. At our May meeting Mr. Wibird was desired to preach a sermon previous to the choice, which he did to great acceptation. The debates were not who, but how many should be sent. They agreed upon three: Mr. Bass for the upper precinct, Colonel Thayer for the middle, and an uncle of ours for this; but he begged to be excused as his state of health was so infirm, and so subject to a nervous headache that he was sure he could not stand it to sit in so numerous an assembly. The next vote was for your brother, and a tie took place between him and Colonel Palmer; but the latter declaring that he would tarry in the House if chosen there, the vote fell upon him.

The disagreeable news we have from Quebec is a great damper to our spirits, but shall we receive good and not evil? Upon this occasion you will recollect the sentiments of your favorite, Sully: "Without attempting to judge of the future, which depends upon too many accidents, much less to subject it to our precipitation in bold and difficult enterprises, we should endeavor to subdue one obstacle at a time, nor suffer ourselves to be depressed by their greatness and their number. We ought never to despair at *what has once been accomplished*. How many things have had the idea of impossible annexed to them, that have become easy to those who knew how to take advantage of time, opportunity, lucky moments, the faults of others, different dispositions and an infinite number of other circumstances."

These are sentiments worthy of the man who could execute what he planned. I sincerely wish we had the spirit of Sully animating our counsels.

27 May

My heart is as light as a feather and my spirits are dancing. I received this afternoon a fine parcel of letters and papers by Colonel Thayer. It was a feast to me. I shall rest in quiet, I hope, this night. The papers I have not read, but sit down to write you, for Mr. Bass has just been here to let me know that Harry will call upon him to-morrow and take this letter for me. I would not have you anxious about me. I make out better than I did.

I have hired a negro fellow for six months, am to give him ten pounds, which is much lower than I had any prospect of getting help, and Belcher is exceedingly assiduous and I believe faithful in what he undertakes. If he should purloin a little I must bear that; he is very diligent, and being chief engineer is ambitious. If you could find a few moments leisure just to write him a few lines and let him know that I had wrote you that he had the care of the place, and that you should be glad of his best services upon it, of his constant care and attention, I believe it would go a good way towards insuring it.

You will find by one of the letters which I mention as having sent an account of some of your affairs. My best endeavors will not be wanting in every department. I wish my abilities were equal to my wishes. My father and your mother desire to be remembered to you in very particular terms. The family you mention are well. So is your brother's; your own are tolerably comfortable. Charles has the mumps and has been very sick but is now better. Can you tell how I feel when they come to me as the two youngest often do, with a *mar,* when will *par* come home? Charley's grandmamma tells this story of him. She was carrying him to meeting the Sabbath the regulars left Boston when a person stopped her upon the road to tell her the news. Gone from Boston says he with his eyes just ready to run over. "What gone away themselves?" "Yes," replied his grandmamma. "Then I say they are cowards, for they have stood it but one year and we would have stood it three."

I took a ride last week, and ventured just as far as the stump of Liberty Tree. Roxbury looks more injured than Boston. That is, the houses look more torn to pieces. I was astonished at the extent of our lines and their strength.

We have taken a most noble prize, the inventory of which you will have in the paper. The poor Captain has since lost his life in a desperate engagement with thirteen boats from the men-of-war, which attacked and attempted to board him; but by a most brave resistance they sunk four of the boats and fought so warmly with their spears and small arms as to oblige them to quit him, though he had but twenty-seven men and they five times his number. He unhappily fell, and was the only one who did. Many dead bodies have since been taken up, among whom is an officer.

We have now in fair sight of my uncle's the commodore, a thirty-six gun frigate, another large vessel, and six small craft. I hope after election we shall have ways and means devised to drive off these torments. Providence seems to have delivered into our hands the very articles most needed, and at a time when we were weak and not so well provided for as we could wish. We have two row-galleys building, and men of spirit to use them I dare say will be found. One engagement only whets their appetite for another.

I heard last night that we had three regiments coming back to us, with General Gates to head them; at which I most sincerely rejoiced. I think he is the man we want. Believe you may venture letters safely by the post. Mine go that way, and for the future I will send to the post-office for yours.

You ask my advice with regard to your office. If I was to consult only my own private satisfaction and pleasure, I should request you to resign it; but alas, that is of small moment when compared to the whole, and I think you qualified and know you disposed to serve your country. I must advise you to hold it, at least for the present year. And in saying this I make a sacrifice which those only can judge of whose hearts are one.

I was much affected, the other day, by a letter which I saw from the lady of the late worthy General Montgomery. Speaking of him, she says, "Suffer me to repeat his last words to me: 'You shall never blush for your Montgomery.' Nobly has he kept his word. As a wife I must ever mourn the husband, friend, and lover of a thousand virtues, of all domestic bliss, the idol of my warmest affections, and, in one word, my every dream of happiness. Methinks I am like the poor widow in the Gospel; having given my mite, I sit down disconsolate."

These are only detached parts of the letter, to which I fear I have not done justice, as I have only my memory to serve me; but it was a very fine letter. Our worthy friends are in great trouble, their eldest son is disordered in his mind. I have not had a line since he was carried home, and I know not the cause. I want to hear from them, but know not how to write to them. I bid you good-night. Oh that I could annihilate space.

Yours.

You have been misinformed. The regulars have not made any fortifications anywhere. It was so reported but was not true. The season promises very fair for grass, and a fine bloom upon the trees. Warm weather we want, which will make everything look finely. I wish you could be here to enjoy it.

24. John Adams

2 June 1776

YESTERDAY I DINED with Captain Richards, the gentleman who made me the present of the brass pistols. We had cherries, strawberries, and green peas in plenty. The fruits are three weeks earlier here than with you. Indeed, they are a fortnight earlier on the east than on the west side of Delaware River. We have had green peas this week past, but they were brought over the river, from New Jersey, to this market. There are none grown in the city or on the west side of the river yet. The reason is, the soil of New Jersey is a warm sand; that of Pennsylvania a cold clay. So much for peas and berries.

Now for something of more importance. In all the correspondence I have maintained, during a course of twenty years, at least, that I have been a writer of letters, I never kept a single copy. This negligence and inaccuracy has been a great misfortune to me on many occasions. I have now purchased a folio book, in the first page of which, expecting one blank leaf, I am writing this letter, and intend to write all my letters to you in it, from this time forward. This will be an advantage to me in several respects. In the first place, I shall write more deliberately. In the second place, I shall be able, at all times, to review what I have written. Third, I shall know how often I write. Fourth, I shall discover by this means whether any of my letters to you miscarry. If it were possible for me to find a conveyance, I would send you such another blank book as a present, that you might begin the practice at the same time, for I really think that your letters are much better worth preserving than mine. Your daughter and sons will very soon write so good hands that they will copy the letters for you from your book, which will improve them, at the same time that it relieves you.

25. Abigail Adams

3 June 1776

I RECEIVED BY Mr. Church a few lines from you. I wish to hear from you every opportunity, though you say no more than that you are well. I feel concerned lest your clothes should go to rags, having nobody to take any care of you in your long absence; and then, you have not with you a proper change for the seasons. However, you must do the best you can. I have a suit of homespun for you whenever you return. I cannot avoid sometimes repining that the gifts of fortune were not bestowed upon us, that I might have enjoyed the happiness of spending my days with my partner, but as it is, I think it my duty to attend with frugality and economy to our own private affairs; and if I cannot add to our little substance, yet see it that it is not diminished. I should enjoy but little comfort in a state of idleness and uselessness. Here I can serve my partner, my family, and myself, and enjoy the satisfaction of your serving your country.

I wish you would write me what I had best do with our house at Boston. I would advertise it if you think best. There are so many houses torn to pieces and so many others abused, that I might stand a chance of letting it, perhaps, as it is in so good repair.

My brother is desirous of joining the army again, but would choose to be a field-officer. I have mentioned him to some of the House, and suppose he will be recommended to Congress for a commission. I hardly know where you will find men to form the regiments required. I begin to think population a very important branch in the American manufactories.

I inclose a list of the Council. The House consists of more than two hundred and fifty members. Your former pupil Angier comes from Bridgewater, and five others. I hope they will proceed in business with a little more spirit than heretofore. They are procuring two row-galleys, but when they will be finished I know not. I thought they were near done, but find to-day they are not yet contracted for. All our gentry are gone from Nantasket Road except the commodore and one or two small craft.

Everything bears a very great price. The merchant complains of the farmer and the farmer of the merchant—both are extravagant. Living is double what it was one year ago.

I find you have licensed tea, but I am determined not to be a purchaser unless I can have it at Congress price, and in that article the venders pay no regard to Congress, asking ten, eight, and the lowest is seven and sixpence per pound. I should like a little green, but they say there is none to be had here. I only wish it for a medicine, as a relief to a nervous pain in my head to which I am sometimes subject. Were it as plenty as ever, I would not practice the use of it.

Our family are all well. It has been reported here that Congress were going to remove forty miles beyond Philadelphia. I gave no credit to the report. I heard no reason assigned for it. I had much rather they would come a hundred miles nearer here.

Adieu.   Yours.

26. John Adams

YESTERDAY WAS TO me a lucky day, as it brought me two letters from you. One dated May 27, and the other June 3d. Don't be concerned about me, if it happens now and then that you don't hear from me for some weeks together. If anything should injure my health materially, you will soon hear of it. But I thank God I am in much better health than I expected to be. But this cannot last long under the load that I carry. When it becomes too great for my strength, I shall ask leave to lay it down, and come home. But I will hold it out a good while yet, if I can. I am willing to take the woodland sister mentions, and the watch and the sword. As to the lighter, it cost more than five hundred dollars in hard cash.

I wish your uncle had as much ambition as he has virtue and ability. A deficiency of ambition is as criminal and injurious as an excess of it. Tell him I say so. How shall we contrive to make so wise and good a man ambitious? Is it not a sin to be so modest? Ask him how he can answer it? So! Then it seems the brigadier was obliged to step downstairs in order to keep my brother out of the lower room. . . . I am sorry for it. Thanks for your quotation from Sully. It is extremely apropos. I am very glad you are so well provided with help. Give my respects to Mr. Belcher and his family. Tell him I am obliged to him for his kind care of the farm. I wish I could go out with him and see the business go on, but I can't. Thank your father and my mother for their kind remembrance of me. Return my duty to both. Charles's young heroism charms me. Kiss him. Poor Mugford, yet glorious Mugford. How beautiful and sublime it is to die for one's country! What a fragrant memory remains!

The rumor you heard of General Gates will prove premature. I endeavored both here and with the General to have it so, and should have succeeded, if it had not been for the loss of General Thomas. Cruel small-pox! worse than the sword! But now, I fear we must part with Gates for the sake of Canada. Mrs. Montgomery is a lady, like all the family, of refined sentiments and elegant accomplishments. Her letter, as you quote it, is very pathetic. Do you mean that our Plymouth friends are in trouble for a disordered son! If so, I am grieved to the heart. God grant them support under so severe an affliction. But this world is a scene of afflictions. I rejoice to hear that the enemy have not fortified, and hope they will not be suffered to attempt it.

Don't think about my clothes. I do well enough in that respect. As to your house at Boston, do with it as you please. Sell it, if you will, but not for a farthing less than it cost me. Let it, if you please, but take care who your tenant is, both of his prudence to preserve the house and his ability to pay the rent. Your brother, I hope will be promoted. He is fit for it, and has deserved it. If his name comes recommended from the General Court, he will have a commission for a field-officer, and I will recommend him to the General for his notice. My pupil, if he pleases, will do Honor to his preceptor, and important service to his country. I hope his zeal and fidelity will be found equal to his abilities.

I send you all the news in the papers. Great things are on the tapis. These throes will usher in the birth of a fine boy. We have no thoughts of removing from hence. There is no occasion for it.

27. Abigail Adams

Plymouth, 17 June 1776, a remarkable day

I THIS DAY received by the hands of our worthy friend a large packet, which has refreshed and comforted me. Your own sensations have ever been similar to mine. I need not then tell you how gratified I am at the frequent tokens of remembrance with which you favor me, nor how they rouse every tender sensation of my soul, which sometimes will find vent at my eyes. Nor dare I describe how earnestly I long to fold to my fluttering heart the object of my warmest affections; the idea soothes me. I feast upon it with a pleasure known only to those whose hearts and hopes are one.

The approbation you give to my conduct in the management of our private affairs is very grateful to me, and sufficiently compensates for all my anxieties and endeavors to discharge the many duties devolved upon me in consequence of the absence of my dearest friend. Were they discharged according to my wishes, I should merit the praises you bestow.

You see I date from Plymouth. I came upon a visit to our amiable friends, accompanied by my sister Betsey, a day or two ago. It is the first night I have been absent since you left me. Having determined upon this visit for some time, I put my family in order and prepared for it, thinking I might leave it with safety. Yet, the day I set out I was under many apprehensions, by the coming in of ten transports, which were seen to have many soldiers on board, and the determination of the people to go and fortify upon Long Island, Pettick's Island, Nantasket, and Great Hill. It was apprehended they would attempt to land somewhere, but the next morning I had the pleasure to hear they were all driven out, commodore and all; not a transport, a ship, or a tender to be seen. This shows what might have been long ago done. Had this been done in season, the ten transports, with many others, in all probability would have fallen into our hands; but the progress of wisdom is slow.

Since I arrived here I have really had a scene quite novel to me. The brig *Defence,* from Connecticut, put in here for ballast. The officers, who are all from thence, and who are intimately acquainted at Dr. Lothrop's, invited his lady to come on board, and bring with her as many of her friends as she could collect. She sent an invitation to our friend, Mrs. Warren, and to us. The brig lay about a mile and a half from town. The officers sent their barge, and we went. Every mark of respect and attention which was in their power, they showed us. She is a fine brig, mounts sixteen guns, twelve swivels, and carries one hundred and twenty men. A hundred and seventeen were on board, and no private family ever appeared under better regulation than the crew. It was as still as though there had been only half a dozen; not a profane word among any of them. The captain himself is an exemplary man (Harden his name); has been in nine sea engagements; says if he gets a man who swears, and finds he cannot reform him, he turns him on shore, yet is free to confess that it was the sin of his youth. He has one lieutenant, a very fine fellow, Smelden by name. We spent a very agreeable afternoon, and drank tea on board. They showed us their arms, which were sent by Queen Anne, and everything on board was a curiosity to me. They gave us a mock engagement with an enemy, and the manner of taking a ship. The young folks went upon the quarterdeck and danced. Some of their Jacks played very well upon the violin and German flute. The brig bears the Continental colors, and was fitted out by the Colony of Connecticut. As we set off from the brig, they fired their guns in honor to us, a ceremony I would very readily have dispensed with.

I pity you, and feel for you under all the difficulties you have to encounter. My daily petitions to Heaven for you are that you may have health, wisdom, and fortitude sufficient to carry you through the great and arduous business in which you are engaged, and that your endeavors may be crowned with success. Canada seems a dangerous and ill-fated place. It is reported here that General Thomas is no more, that he took the small-pox, and died with it. Every day some circumstance arises which shows me the importance of having that distemper in youth. Dr. Bulfinch has petitioned the General Court for leave to open a hospital somewhere, and it will be granted him. I shall, with all the children, be one of the first class, you may depend upon it.

I have just this moment heard that the brig which I was on board of on Saturday, and which sailed yesterday morning from this place, fell in with two transports, having each of them a hundred and fifty men on board, and took them, and has brought them into Nantasket Road, under cover of the guns which are mounted there. I will add further particulars as soon as I am informed.

I am now better informed, and will give you the truth. The brig *Defence,* accompanied by a small privateer, sailed in concert Sunday morning. About twelve o'clock they discovered two transports, and made for them. Two privateers, who were small, had been in chase of them, but finding the enemy was of much larger force, had run under Cohasset rocks. The *Defence* gave a signal gun to bring them out. Captain Burk, who accompanied the *Defence,* being a prime sailer, he came up first, and poured a broadside on board a sixteen gun brig. The *Defence* soon attacked her upon her bows. An obstinate engagement ensued. There was a continual blaze upon all sides for many hours, and it was near midnight before they struck. In the engagement, the *Defence* lost one man, and five wounded. With Burk, not one man received any damage; on board the enemy, fourteen killed, among whom was a major, and sixty wounded. They are part of the Highland soldiers. The other transport mounted six guns. When the fleet sailed out of this harbor last week, they blew up the lighthouse. They met six transports coming in, which they carried off with them. I hope we shall soon be in such a posture of defense as to bid them defiance.

I feel no great anxiety at the large armament designed against us. The remarkable interpositions of Heaven in our favor cannot be too gratefully acknowledged. He who fed the Israelites in the wilderness, who clothes the lilies of the field, and feeds the young ravens when they cry, will not forsake a people engaged in so righteous a cause, if we remember his loving-kindness. We wanted powder,—we have a supply. We wanted arms,—we have been favored in that respect. We wanted hard money,—twenty-two thousand dollars, and an equal value in plate, are delivered into our hands.

You mention your peas, your cherries, and your strawberries, etc. Ours are but just in blossom. We have had the coldest spring I ever knew. Things are three weeks back of what they generally used to be. The corn looks poor. The season now is rather dry. Our friend has refused his appointment. I am very sorry. I said everything I could think to persuade him, but his lady was against it. I need say no more. I believe I did not understand you, when in a former letter you said, "I want to resign my office, for a thousand reasons." If you mean that of judge, I know not what to say. I know it will be a difficult and arduous station; but, divesting myself of private interest, which would lead me to be against your holding that office, I know of no person who is so well calculated to discharge the trust, or who I think would act a more conscientious part. My paper is full. I have only room to thank you for it.

28. John Adams

Philadelphia, 26 June 1776

I HAVE WRITTEN so seldom to you, that I am really grieved at the recollection. I wrote you a few lines June 2, and a few more June 16. These are all that I have written to you since this month began. It has been the busiest month that ever I saw. I have found time to inclose all the newspapers, which I hope you will receive in due time.

Our misfortunes in Canada are enough to melt a heart of stone. The small-pox is ten times more terrible than Britons, Canadians, and Indians, together. This was the cause of our precipitate retreat from Quebec. This the cause of our disgraces at the Cedars. I don't mean that this was all. There has been want approaching to famine, as well as pestilence. And these discouragements have so disheartened our officers that none of them seem to act with prudence and firmness. But these reverses of fortune don't discourage me. It was natural to expect them, and we ought to be prepared in our minds for greater changes and more melancholy scenes still. It is an animating cause, and brave spirits are not subdued with difficulties.

Amidst all our gloomy prospects in Canada, we receive some pleasure from Boston. I congratulate you on your victory over your enemies in the harbor. This has long lain near my heart, and it gives me great pleasure to think that what was so much wished is accomplished. I hope our people will now make the lower harbor impregnable, and never again suffer the flag of a tyrant to fly within any part of it.

The Congress have been pleased to give me more business than I am qualified for, and more than, I fear, I can go through, with safety to my health. They have established a board of war and ordnance and made me President of it, an honor to which I never aspired, a trust to which I feel myself vastly unequal. But I am determined to do as well as I can, and make industry supply, in some degree, the place of abilities and experience. The Board sits every morning and every evening. This with constant attendance in Congress will so entirely engross my time, that I fear I shall not be able to write you so often as I have. But I will steal time to write to you.

The small-pox! the small-pox! what shall we do with it? I could almost wish that an inoculating hospital was opened in every town in New England. It is some small consolation that the scoundrel savages have taken a large dose of it. They plundered the baggage and stripped off the clothes of our men who had the small-pox out full upon them at the Cedars.

29. John Adams

3 July 1776

YOUR FAVOR OF 17 June, dated at Plymouth, was handed me by yesterday's post. I was much pleased to find that you had taken a journey to Plymouth, to see your friends, in the long absence of one whom you may wish to see. The excursion will be an amusement, and will serve your health. How happy would it have made me to have taken this journey with you!

I was informed, a day or two before the receipt of your letter, that you was gone to Plymouth, by Mrs. Polly Palmer, who was obliging enough, in your absence, to send me the particulars of the expedition to the lower harbor against the men-of-war. Her narration is executed with a precision and perspicuity, which would have become the pen of an accomplished historian.

I am very glad you had so good an opportunity of seeing one of our little American men-of-war. Many ideas now to you must have presented themselves in such a scene; and you will, in future, better understand the relations of sea engagements.

I rejoice extremely at Dr. Bulfinch's petition to open a hospital. But I hope the business will be done upon a larger scale. I hope that one hospital will be licensed in every county, if not in every town. I am happy to find you resolved to be with the children in the first class. Mr. Whitney and Mrs. Katy Quincy are cleverly through inoculation in this city. I have one favor to ask, and that is, that in your future letters, you would acknowledge the receipt of all those you may receive from me, and mention their dates. By this means I shall know if any of mine miscarry.

The information you give me of our friend's refusing his appointment has given me much pain, grief, and anxiety. I believe I shall be obliged to follow his example. I have not fortune enough to support my family, and, what is of more importance, to support the dignity of that exalted station. It is too high and lifted up for me, who delight in nothing so much as retreat, solitude, silence, and obscurity. In private life, no one has a right to censure me for following my own inclinations in retirement, simplicity, and frugality. In public life, every man has a right to remark as he pleases. At least he thinks so.

Yesterday, the greatest question was decided which ever was debated in America, and a greater, perhaps, never was nor will be decided among men. A Resolution was passed without one dissenting Colony "that these United Colonies are, and of right ought to be, free and independent States, and as such they have, and of right ought to have, full power to make war, conclude peace, establish commerce, and to do all other acts and things which other States may rightfully do." You will see, in a few days, a Declaration setting forth the causes which have impelled us to this mighty revolution, and the reasons which will justify it in the sight of God and man. A plan of confederation will be taken up in a few days.

When I look back to the year 1761, and recollect the argument concerning writs of assistance in the superior court, which I have hitherto considered as the commencement of this controversy between Great Britain and America, and run through the whole period from that time to this, and recollect the series of political events, the chain of causes and effects, I am surprised at the suddenness as well as greatness of this revolution. Britain has been filled with folly, and America with wisdom; at least, this is my judgment. Time must determine. It is the will of Heaven that the two countries should be sundered forever. It may be the will of Heaven that America shall suffer calamities still more wasting, and distresses yet more dreadful. If this is to be the case, it will have this good effect at least. It will inspire us with many virtues which we have not, and correct many errors, follies, and vices which threaten to disturb, dishonor, and destroy us. The furnace of affliction produces refinement in states as well as individuals. And the new Governments we are assuming in every part will require a purification from our vices, and an augmentation of our virtues, or they will be no blessings. The people will have unbounded power, and the people are extremely addicted to corruption and venality, as well as the great. But I must submit all my hopes and fears to an overruling Providence, in which, unfashionable as the faith may be, I firmly believe.

30. John Adams

Philadelphia, 3 July 1776

HAD A DECLARATION of Independency been made seven months ago, it would have been attended with many great and glorious effects. We might, before this hour, have formed alliances with foreign states. We should have mastered Quebec, and been in possession of Canada. You will perhaps wonder how such a declaration would have influenced our affairs in Canada, but if I could write with freedom, I could easily convince you that it would, and explain to you the manner how. Many gentlemen in high stations, and of great influence, have been duped by the ministerial bubble of Commissioners to treat. And in real, sincere expectation of this event, which they so fondly wished, they have been slow and languid in promoting measures for the reduction of that province. Others there are in the Colonies who really wished that our enterprise in Canada would be defeated, that the Colonies might be brought into danger and distress between two fires, and be thus induced to submit. Others really wished to defeat the expedition to Canada, lest the conquest of it should elevate the minds of the people too much to hearken to those terms of reconciliation which, they believed, would be offered us. These jarring views, wishes, and designs occasioned an opposition to many salutary measures which were proposed for the support of that expedition, and caused obstructions, embarrassments, and studied delays, which have finally lost us the province.

All these causes, however, in conjunction would not have disappointed us, if it had not been for a misfortune which could not be foreseen, and perhaps could not have been prevented; I mean the prevalence of the small-pox among our troops. This fatal pestilence completed our destruction. It is a frown of Providence upon us, which we ought to lay to heart.

But, on the other hand, the delay of this Declaration to this time has many great advantages attending it. The hopes of reconciliation which were fondly entertained by multitudes of honest and well-meaning, though weak and mistaken people, have been gradually, and at last totally extinguished. Time has been given for the whole people maturely to consider the great question of independence, and to ripen their judgment, dissipate their fears, and allure their hopes, by discussing it in newspapers and pamphlets, by debating it in assemblies, conventions, committees of safety and inspection, in town and county meetings, as well as in private conversations, so that the whole people, in every colony of the thirteen, have now adopted it as their own act. This will cement the union, and avoid those heats, and perhaps convulsions, which might have been occasioned by such a Declaration six months ago.

But the day is past. The second day of July, 1776, will be the most memorable epocha in the history of America. I am apt to believe that it will be celebrated by succeeding generations as the great anniversary festival. It ought to be commemorated as the day of deliverance, by solemn acts of devotion to God Almighty. It ought to be solemnized with pomp and parade, with shows, games, sports, guns, bells, bonfires, and illuminations, from one end of this continent to the other, from this time forward forever-more.

You will think me transported with enthusiasm, but I am not. I am well aware of the toil and blood and treasure that it will cost us to maintain this Declaration and support and defend these States. Yet, through all the gloom, I can see the rays of ravishing light and glory. I can see that the end is more than worth all the means. And that posterity will triumph in that day's transaction, even although we should rue it, which I trust in God we shall not.

31. John Adams

Philadelphia, 7 July 1776

I HAVE THIS moment folded up a magazine and an "Evening Post," and sent them off by an express who could not wait for me to write a single line. It always goes to my heart to send off a packet of pamphlets and newspapers without a letter, but it sometimes unavoidably happens, and I suppose you had rather receive a pamphlet or newspaper than nothing.

The design of our enemy now seems to be a powerful invasion of New York and New Jersey. The Halifax fleet and army is arrived, and another fleet and army under Lord Howe is expected to join them. We are making great preparations to meet them by marching the militia of Maryland, Pennsylvania, and New Jersey down to the scene of action, and have made large requisitions upon New England. I hope, for the honor of New England and the salvation of America, our people will not be backward in marching to New York. We must maintain and defend that important post, at all events. If the enemy get possession there, it will cost New England very dear. There is no danger of the small-pox at New York. It is carefully kept out of the city and the army. I hope that your brother and mine too will go into the service of their country at this critical period of its distress.

Our army at Crown Point is an object of wretchedness enough to fill a humane mind with horror; disgraced, defeated, discontented, dispirited, diseased, naked, undisciplined, eaten up with vermin, no clothes, beds, blankets, no medicines, no victuals but salt pork and flour. A chaplain from that army preached a sermon here the other day from "Cursed is he that doeth the work of the Lord deceitfully."

I knew, better than he did, who the persons were who deserved these curses. But I could not help myself, nor my poor country, any more than he. I hope that measures will be taken to cleanse the army at Crown Point from the small-pox, and that other measures will be taken in New England, by tolerating and encouraging inoculation, to render that distemper less terrible.

I am solicitous to hear what figure our new Superior Court made in their eastern circuit; what business they did; whether the grand juries and petit juries were sworn; whether they tried any criminals, or any civil actions; how the people were affected at the appearance of Courts again; how the judges were treated; whether with respect or cold neglect, etc. Every colony upon the continent will soon be in the same situation. They are erecting governments as fast as children build cob-houses; but, I conjecture, they will hardly throw them down again so soon.

The practice we have hitherto been in, of ditching round about our enemies, will not always do. We must learn to use other weapons than the pick and the spade. Our armies must be disciplined, and learn to fight. I have the satisfaction to reflect that our Massachusetts people, when they have been left to themselves, have been constantly fighting and skirmishing, and always with success. I wish the same valor, prudence, and spirit had been discovered everywhere.

32. John Adams

Philadelphia, 7 July 1776

IT IS WORTH the while of a person, obliged to write as much as I do, to consider the varieties of style. The epistolary is essentially different from the oratorical and the historical style. Oratory abounds with figures. History is simple, but grave, majestic, and formal. Letters, like conversation, should be free, easy, and familiar. Simplicity and familiarity are the characteristics of this kind of writing. Affectation is as disagreeable in a letter as in conversation, and therefore studied language, premeditated method, and sublime sentiments are not expected in a letter. Notwithstanding which, the sublime, as well as the beautiful and the novel, may naturally enough appear in familiar letters among friends. Among the ancients there are two illustrious examples of the epistolary style, Cicero and Pliny, whose letters present you with models of fine writing, which have borne the criticism of almost two thousand years. In these you see the sublime, the beautiful, the novel, and the pathetic, conveyed in as much simplicity, ease, freedom, and familiarity as language is capable of.

Let me request you to turn over the leaves of "The Preceptor" to a letter of Pliny the Younger, in which he has transmitted to these days the history of his uncle's philosophical curiosity, his heroic courage, and his melancholy catastrophe. Read it, and say whether it is possible to write a narrative of facts in a better manner. It is copious and particular in selecting the circumstances most natural, remarkable, and affecting. There is not an incident omitted which ought to have been remembered, nor one inserted that is not worth remembrance. It gives you an idea of the scene, as distinct and perfect as if a painter had drawn it to the life before your eyes. It interests your passions as much as if you had been an eye-witness of the whole transaction. Yet there are no figures or art used. All is as simple, natural, easy, and familiar as if the story had been told in conversation, without a moment's premeditation.

Pope and Swift have given the world a collection of their letters; but I think in general they fall short, in the epistolary way, of their own eminence in poetry and other branches of literature. Very few of their letters have ever engaged much of my attention. Gay's letter concerning the pair of lovers killed by lightning is worth more than the whole collection, in point of simplicity and elegance of composition, and as a genuine model of the epistolary style. There is a book, which I wish you owned,—I mean Rollin's "Belles Lettres,"—in which the variations of style are explained.

Early youth is the time to learn the arts and sciences, and especially to correct the ear and the imagination, by forming a style. I wish you would think of forming the taste and judgment of your children now, before any unchaste sounds have fastened on their ears, and before any affectation or vanity is settled on their minds, upon the pure principles of nature. Music is a great advantage; for style depends, in part, upon a delicate ear. The faculty of writing is attainable by art, practice, and habit only. The sooner, therefore, the practice begins, the more likely it will be to succeed. Have no mercy upon an affected phrase, any more than an affected air, gait, dress, or manners.

Your children have capacities equal to anything. There is a vigor in the understanding and a spirit and fire in the temper of every one of them, which is capable of ascending the heights of art, science, trade, war, or politics. They should be set to compose descriptions of scenes and objects, and narrations of facts and events. Declamations upon topics and other exercises of various sorts should be prescribed to them. Set a child to form a description of a battle, a storm, a siege, a cloud, a mountain, a lake, a city, a harbor, a country seat, a meadow, a forest, or almost anything that may occur to your thoughts. Set him to compose a narration of all the little incidents and events of a day, a journey, a ride, or a walk. In this way a taste will be formed, and a facility of writing acquired.

For myself, as I never had a regular tutor, I never studied anything methodically, and consequently never was completely accomplished in anything. But, as I am conscious of my own deficiency in these respects, I should be the less pardonable if I neglected the education of my children. In grammar, rhetoric, logic, my education was imperfect, because immethodical. Yet I have perhaps read more upon these arts, and considered them in a more extensive view, than some others.

33. John Adams

10 July

YOU WILL SEE, by the newspapers which I from time to time inclose, with what rapidity the colonies proceed in their political manoeuvres. How many calamities might have been avoided if these measures had been taken twelve months ago, or even no longer ago than last December?

The colonies to the south are pursuing the same maxima which have heretofore governed those to the north. In constituting their new governments, their plans are remarkably popular, more so than I could ever have imagined; even more popular than the "Thoughts on Government"; and in the choice of their rulers, capacity, spirit, and zeal in the cause supply the place of fortune, family, and every other consideration which used to have weight with mankind. My friend Archibald Bullock, Esquire, is Governor of Georgia. John Rutledge, Esquire, is Governor of South Carolina. Patrick Henry, Esquire, is Governor of Virginia, etc. Dr. Franklin will be Governor of Pennsylvania. The new members of this city are all in this taste, chosen because of their inflexible zeal for independence. All the old members left out because they opposed independence, or at least were lukewarm about it. Dickinson, Morris, Allen, all fallen, like grass before the scythe, notwithstanding all their vast advantages in point of fortune, family, and abilities. I am inclined to think, however, and to wish, that these gentlemen may be restored at a fresh election, because, although mistaken in some points, they are good characters, and their great wealth and numerous connections will contribute to strengthen America and cement her union.

I wish I were at perfect liberty to portray before you all these characters in their genuine lights, and to explain to you the course of political changes in this province. It would give you a great idea of the spirit and resolution of the people, and show you, in a striking point of view, the deep roots of American independence in all the colonies. But it is not prudent to commit to writing such free speculations in the present state of things. Time, which takes away the veil, may lay open the secret springs of this surprising revolution. But I find, although the colonies have differed in religion, laws, customs, and manners, yet in the great essentials of society and government they are all alike.

34. John Adams

Philadelphia, 11 July 1776

You seem to be situated in the place of greatest tranquillity and security of any upon the continent. I may be mistaken in this particular, and an armament may have invaded your neighborhood, before now. But we have no intelligence of any such design, and all that we now know of the motions, plans, operations, and designs of the enemy indicates the contrary. It is but just that you should have a little rest, and take a little breath.

I wish I knew whether your brother and mine have enlisted in the army, and what spirit is manifested by our militia for marching to New York and Crown Point. The militia of Maryland, New Jersey, Pennsylvania, and the lower counties are marching with much alacrity, and a laudable zeal to take care of Howe and his army at Staten Island. The army in New York is in high spirits, and seems determined to give the enemy a serious reception. The unprincipled and unfeeling and unnatural inhabitants of Staten Island are cordially receiving the enemy, and, deserters say, have engaged to take arms. They are an ignorant, cowardly pack of scoundrels. Their numbers are small, and their spirit less.

It is some time since I received any letter from you. The Plymouth one was the last. You must write me every week, by the post, if it is but a few lines. It gives me many spirits. I design to write to the General Court requesting a dismission, or at least a furlough. I think to propose that they choose four more members, or at least three more, that so we may attend here in rotation. Two or three or four may be at home at a time, and the Colony properly represented notwithstanding. Indeed, while the Congress were employed in political regulations, forming the sentiments of the people of the Colonies into some consistent system, extinguishing the remainders of authority under the crown, and gradually erecting and strengthening governments under the authority of the people, turning their thoughts upon the principles of polity and the forms of government, framing constitutions for the Colonies separately, and a limited and a defined Confederacy for the United Colonies, and in some other measures, which I do not choose to mention particularly, but which are now determined, or near the point of determination, I flattered myself that I might have been of some little use here. But now, these matters will be soon completed, and very little business will be to be done here but what will be either military or commercial; branches of knowledge and business for which hundreds of others in our province are much better qualified than I am. I shall therefore request my masters to relieve me.

I am not a little concerned about my health, which seems to have been providentially preserved to me, much beyond my expectations. But I begin to feel the disagreeable effects of unremitting attention to business for so long a time, and a want of exercise, and the bracing quality of my native air; so that I have the utmost reason to fear an irreparable injury to my constitution, if I do not obtain a little relaxation. The fatigues of war are much less destructive to health than the painful, laborious attention to debates and to writing, which drinks up the spirits and consumes the strength.   I am, etc.

35. Abigail Adams

I MUST BEGIN with apologizing to you for not writing since the 17th of June. I have really had so many cares upon my hands and mind, with a bad inflammation in my eyes, that I have not been able to write. I now date from Boston, where I yesterday arrived and was with all of our little ones inoculated for the small-pox. My uncle and aunt were so kind as to send me an invitation with my family. Mr. Cranch and wife and family, my sister Betsey and her little niece, Cotton Tufts and Mr. Thaxter, a maid who has had the distemper and my old nurse compose our family. A boy too I should have added. Seventeen in all. My uncle's maid with his little daughter and a negro man are here. We had our bedding, etc., to bring. A cow we have driven down from Braintree and some hay I have had put into the stable, wood, etc., and we have really commenced housekeepers here. The house was furnished with almost every article (except beds), which we have free use of, and think ourselves much obliged by the fine accommodations and kind offer of our friends. All our necessary stores we purchase jointly. Our little ones stood the operation manfully. Dr. Bulfinch is our physician. Such a spirit of inoculation never before took place; the town and every house in it are as full as they can hold. I believe there are not less than thirty persons from Braintree. Mrs. Quincy, Mrs. Lincoln, Miss Betsy, and Nancy are our near neighbors. God grant that we may all go comfortably through the distemper; the physic part is bad enough I know. I knew your mind so perfectly upon the subject that I thought nothing but our recovery would give you equal pleasure, and as to safety there was none. The soldiers inoculated privately, so did many of the inhabitants and the paper currency spread it everywhere. I immediately determined to set myself about it, and get ready with my children. I wish it was so you could have been with us, but I submit. I received some letters from you last Saturday night the 26th of June. You mention a letter of the 16th which I have never received, and I suppose must relate something to private affairs which I wrote about in May and sent by Harry.

As to news, we have taken several prizes since I wrote you, as you will see by the newspapers. The present report is of Lord Howe's coming with unlimited powers. However, suppose it is so, I believe he little thinks of treating with us as Independent States. How can any person yet dream of a settlement, accommodations, etc.? They have neither the spirit nor the feeling of men. Yet I see some who never were called Tories gratified with the idea of Lord Howe's being upon his passage with such powers!

Sunday, 14 July

By yesterday's post I received two letters dated 3d and 4th of July, and though your letters never fail to give me pleasure, be the subject what it will, yet it was greatly heightened by the prospect of the future happiness and glory of our country. Nor am I a little gratified when I reflect that a person so nearly connected with me has had the honor of being a principal actor in laying a foundation for its future greatness.

May the foundation of our new Constitution be Justice, Truth, and Righteousness! Like the wise man's house, may it be founded upon these rocks, and then neither storms nor tempests will over-throw it!

I cannot but feel sorry that some of the most manly sentiments in the Declaration are expunged from the printed copy. Perhaps wise reasons induced it.

Poor Canada, I lament Canada, but we ought to be in some measure sufferers for the past folly of our conduct. The fatal effects of the small-pox there has led almost every person to consent to hospitals in every town. In many towns already around Boston the selectmen have granted liberty for inoculation. I hope the necessity is now fully seen. I had many disagreeable sensations at the thoughts of coming myself, but to see my children through it I thought my duty, and all those feelings vanished as soon as I was inoculated, and I trust a kind

Providence will carry me safely through. Our friends from Plymouth came into town yesterday. We have enough upon our hands in the morning. The little folks are very sick then and puke every morning but after that they are comfortable.

I shall write you now very often. Pray inform me constantly of every important action. Every expression of tenderness is a cordial to my heart. Important as they are to the rest of the world, to me they are *everything*.

We have had during all the month of June a most severe drought, which cut off all our promising hopes of English grain and the first crop of grass, but since July came in we have had a plenty of rain and now everything looks well. There is one misfortune in our family which I have never mentioned in hopes it would have been in my power to have remedied it, but all hopes of that kind are at an end. It is the loss of your gray horse. About two months ago, I had occasion to send Jonathan of an errand to my uncle Quincy's (the other horse being a plowing). Upon his return a little below the church she trod upon a rolling stone and lamed herself to that degree that it was with great difficulty that she could be got home. I immediately sent for Tirrell, and everything was done for her by baths, ointments, polticing, bleeding, etc., that could be done. Still she continued extremely lame, though not so bad as at first. I then got her carried to Domet, but he pronounces her incurable, as a callus is grown upon her fetlock joint. She was not with foal, as you imagined, but I hope she is now as care has been taken in that respect.

I suppose you have heard of a fleet which came up pretty near the Light and kept us all with our mouths open, ready to catch them, but after staying near a week, and making what observations they could, set sail and went off to our great mortification, who were [?] for them in every respect. If our ship of thirty-two guns which was built at Portsmouth, and waiting only for guns, and another at Plymouth in the same state, had been in readiness, we should in all probability have been masters of them. Where the blame lies in that respect, I know not. 'Tis laid upon Congress, and Congress is also blamed for not appointing us a General. But Rome was not built in a day.

I hope the multiplicity of cares and avocations which envelop you will not be too powerful for you. I have many anxieties upon that account. Nabby and Johnny send duty and desire mamma to say that an inflammation in their eyes, which has been as much of a distemper as the small-pox, has prevented their writing, but they hope soon to be able to acquaint papa of their happy recovery from the distemper.

Mr. Cranch and wife, sister Betsey, and all our friends desire to be remembered to you, and foremost in that number stands your   PORTIA

A little India herb would have been mighty agreeable now.

36. John Adams

MY VERY DESERVING friend, Mr. Gerry, sets off to-morrow for Boston, worn out of health by the fatigues of this station. He is an excellent man, and an active, able statesman. I hope he will soon return hither. I am sure I should be glad to return with him, but I cannot. I must wait to have the guard relieved.

There is a most amiable, laudable, and gallant spirit prevailing in these middle colonies. The militia turn out in great numbers and in high spirits, in New Jersey, Pennsylvania, Maryland, and Delaware, so that we hope to resist Howe and his myrmidons.

Independence is, at last, unanimously agreed to in the New York Convention. You will see, by the newspapers inclosed, what is going forward in Virginia and Maryland and New Jersey. Farewell! farewell! infatuated, besotted step-dame. I have not time to add more than that I receive letters from you but seldom of late. To-morrow's post, I hope, will bring me some. So I hoped of last Saturday's and last Tuesday's.

37. John Adams

20 July

I CANNOT OMIT the opportunity of writing you a line by this post. This letter will, I suppose, find you, in some degree or other, under the influence of the small-pox. The air is of very great importance. I don't know your physician, but I hope he won't deprive you of air more than is necessary.

We had yesterday an express from General Lee in Charleston, South Carolina, with an account of a brilliant little action between the armament under Clinton and Cornwallis, and a battery on Sullivan's Island, which terminated very fortunately for America. I will endeavor to inclose with this a printed account of it. It has given us good spirits here, and will have a happy effect upon our armies at New York and Ticonderoga. Surely our northern soldiers will not suffer themselves to be outdone by their brethren so nearly under the sun. I don't yet hear of any Massachusetts men at New York. Our people must not flinch at this critical moment, when their country is in more danger than it ever will be again, perhaps. What will they say if the Howes should prevail against our forces at so important a post as New York, for want of a few thousand men from the Massachusetts? I will likewise send you by this post Lord Howe's letter and proclamation, which has let the cat out of the bag. These tricks deceive no longer. Gentlemen here, who either were or pretended to be deceived heretofore, now see or pretend to see through such artifices. I apprehend his Lordship is afraid of being attacked upon Staten Island, and is throwing out his barrels to amuse Leviathan until his reinforcements shall arrive.

20 July

This has been a dull day to me. I waited the arrival of the post with much solicitude and impatience, but his arrival made me more solicitous still. "To be left at the Post Office," in your handwriting on the back of a few lines from the Dr. was all that I could learn of you and my little folks. If you was too busy to write, I hoped that some kind hand would have been found to let me know something about you. Do my friends think that I have been a politician so long as to have lost all feeling? Do they suppose I have forgotten my wife and children? Or are they so panic-struck with the loss of Canada as to be afraid to correspond with me? Or have they forgotten that you have a husband, and your children a father? What have I done, or omitted to do, that I should be thus forgotten and neglected in the most tender and affecting scene of my life? Don't mistake me. I don't blame you. Your time and thoughts must have been wholly taken up with your own and your family's situation and necessities; but twenty other persons might have informed me.

I suspect that you intended to have run slyly through the small-pox with the family, without letting me know it, and then have sent me an account that you were all well. This might be a kind intention, and if the design had succeeded, would have made me very joyous. But the secret is out, and I am left to conjecture. But as the faculty have this distemper so much under command, I will flatter myself with the hope and expectation of soon hearing of your recovery.

38. Abigail Adams

Boston, 21 July 1776

I HAVE NO doubt that my dearest friend is anxious to know how his Portia does, and his little flock of children under the operation of a disease once so formidable. I have the pleasure to tell him that they are all comfortable, though some of them complaining. Nabby has been very ill, but the eruption begins to make its appearance upon her, and upon Johnny. Tommy is so well that the Dr. inoculated him again today fearing that it had not taken. Charley has no complaints yet, though his arm has been very sore.

I have been out to meeting this forenoon, but have so many disagreeable sensations this afternoon that I thought it prudent to tarry at home. The Dr. says they are very good feelings. Mr. Cranch has passed through the preparation, and the eruption is coming out cleverly upon him without any sickness at all. Mrs. Cranch is cleverly and so are all her children. Those who are broke out are pretty full for the new method, as 'tis called the Suttonian they profess to practice upon. I hope to give you a good account when I write next, but our eyes are very weak and the Dr. is not fond of either writing or reading for his patients. But I must transgress a little.

I received a letter from you by Wednesday's post, the 7th of July, and though I think it is a choice one in the literary way, containing many useful hints and judicious observations which will greatly assist me in the future instruction of the little ones, yet it lacked some essential ingredients to make it compleat. Not one word respecting yourself, your health or your present situation. My anxiety for your welfare will never leave me but with my parting breath, 'tis of more importance to me than all this world contains besides. The cruel separation to which I am necessitated cuts off half the enjoyments of life, the other half are comprised in the hope I have that what I do and what I suffer may be serviceable to you, to our little ones and our country. I must beseech you therefore for the future never to omit what is so essential to my happiness.

Last Thursday, after hearing a very good sermon, I went with the multitude into King Street to hear the Proclamation for Independence read and proclaimed. Some field-pieces with the train were brought there. The troops appeared under arms, and all the inhabitants assembled there (the small-pox prevented many thousand from the country), when Colonel Crafts read from the balcony of the State House the proclamation. Great attention was given to every word. As soon as he ended, the cry from the balcony was, "God save our American States," and then three cheers which rended the air. The bells rang, the privateers fired, the forts and batteries, the cannon were discharged, the platoons followed, and every face appeared joyful. Mr. Bowdoin then gave a sentiment, "Stability and perpetuity to American independence." After dinner, the King's Arms were taken down from the State House, and every vestige of him from every place in which it appeared, and burnt in King Street. Thus ends royal authority in this State. And all the people shall say, Amen.

I have been a little surprised that we collect no better accounts with regard to the horrid conspiracy at New York, and that so little mention has been made of it here. It made a talk for a few days, but now seems all hushed in silence. The Tories say that it was not a conspiracy, but an association. And pretend that there was no plot to assassinate the General. Even their hardened hearts feel the discovery we have in George a match for a Borgia or a Catiline, a wretch callous to every humane feeling. Our worthy preacher told us that he believed one of our great sins, for which a righteous God has come out in judgment against us, was our bigoted attachment to so wicked a man. May our repentance be sincere.

I omitted many things yesterday in order to be better informed. I have got Mr. Cranch to inquire and write you, concerning a French schooner from Martinique which came in yesterday and a prize from Ireland. My own infirmities prevent my writing. A most excruciating pain in my head and every limb and joint I hope portends a speedy eruption and prevents my saying more than that I am forever yours. The children are not yet broke out. 'Tis the eleventh day with us.

39. John Adams

29 July

How ARE YOU all this morning? Sick, weak, faint, in pain, or pretty well recovered? By this time, you are well acquainted with the small-pox. Pray, how do you like it?

We have no news. It is very hard that half a dozen or half a score armies can't supply us with news. We have a famine, a perfect dearth of this necessary article. I am, at this present writing, perplexed and plagued with two knotty problems in politics. You love to pick a political bone. So I will even throw it to you.

If a confederation should take place, one great question is, how we shall vote. Whether each colony shall count one; or whether each shall have a weight in proportion to its numbers, or wealth, or exports and imports, or a compound ratio of all. Another is, whether Congress shall have authority to limit the dimensions of each colony, to prevent those, which claim by charter, or proclamation, or commission to the south sea, from growing too great and powerful, so as to be dangerous to the rest?

Shall I write you a sheet upon each of these questions? When you are well enough to read, and I can find leisure enough to write, perhaps I may.

Gerry carried with him a canister for you. But he is an old bachelor, and what is worse, a politician, and what is worse still, a kind of soldier; so that I suppose he will have so much curiosity to see armies and fortifications, and assemblies, that you will lose many a fine breakfast at a time when you want them most.

Tell Betsey that this same Gerry is such another as herself, sex excepted. How is my brother and friend Cranch? How is his other self and their little selves, and ours? Don't be in the dumps, above all things. I am hard put to it to keep out of them, when I look at home. But I will be gay if I can.   Adieu.

40. John Adams

THE POST WAS later than usual to-day, so that I had not yours of July 24 till this evening. You have made me very happy by the particular and favorable account you give me of all the family. But I don't understand how there are so many who have no eruptions and no symptoms. The inflammation in the arm might do, but without these there is no small-pox. I will lay a wager, that your whole hospital has not had so much small-pox as Mrs. Katy Quincy. Upon my word, she has had an abundance of it, but is finally recovered, looks as fresh as a rose, but pitted all over as thick as ever you saw any one. I this evening presented your compliments and thanks to Mr. Hancock for his polite offer of his house, and likewise your compliments to his lady and Mrs. Katy.

4 August

Went this morning to the Baptist meeting, in hopes of hearing Mr. Stillman, but was disappointed. He was there, but another gentleman preached. His action was violent to a degree bordering on fury; his gestures unnatural and distorted. Not the least idea of grace in his motions, or elegance in his style. His voice was vociferous and boisterous, and his composition almost wholly destitute of ingenuity. I wonder extremely at the fondness of our people for scholars educated at the southward, and for southern preachers. There is no one thing in which we excel them more than in our University, our scholars and preachers. Particular gentlemen here, who have improved upon their education by travel, shine; but in general, old Massachusetts outshines her younger sisters. Still in several particulars they have more wit than we. They have societies, the Philosophical Society particularly, which excites a scientific emulation, and propagates their fame. If ever I got through this scene of politics and war, I will spend the remainder of my days in endeavoring to instruct my countrymen in the art of making the most of their abilities and virtues; an art which they have hitherto too much neglected. A philosophical society shall be established at Boston, if I have wit and address enough to accomplish it, sometime or other. Pray set brother Cranch's philosophical head to plodding upon this project. Many of his lucubrations would have been published and preserved, for the benefit of mankind and for his honor, if such a club had existed.

My countrymen want art and address. They want knowledge of the world. They want the exterior and superficial accomplishment of gentlemen, upon which the world has set so high a value. In solid abilities and real virtues they vastly excel, in general, any people upon this continent. Our New England people are awkward and bashful, yet they are pert, ostentatious, and vain; a mixture which excites ridicule and gives disgust. They have not the faculty of showing themselves to the best advantage, nor the art of concealing this faculty; an art and faculty which some people possess in the highest degree. Our deficiencies in these respects are owing wholly to the little intercourse we have with strangers, and to our inexperience in the world. These imperfections must be remedied, for New England must produce the heroes, the statesmen, the philosophers, or America will make no great figure for some time.

Our army is rather sickly at New York, and we live in daily expectation of hearing of some great event. May God Almighty grant it may be prosperous for America. Hope is an anchor and a cordial. Disappointment, however, will not disconcert us.

If you will come to Philadelphia in September, I will stay as long as you please. I should be as proud and happy as a bridegroom.   Yours.

41. John Adams

Philadelphia, 11 August 1776

MR. A. SETS OFF to-day, if the rain should not prevent him, with Colonel Whipple, of Portsmouth, a brother of the celebrated Miss Hannah Whipple, a sensible and worthy man. By him I have sent you two bundles of letters, which I hope you will be careful of. I thought I should not be likely to find a safer opportunity. By them you will see that my private correspondence alone is business enough for a lazy man. I think I have answered all but a few of those large bundles.

A French vessel, a pretty large brigantine, deeply laden, arrived here yesterday from Martinique. She had fifty barrels of limes, which are all sold already, at such prices that the amount of them will be sufficient to load the brig with flour. The trade, we see, even now, in the midst of summer, is not totally interrupted by all the efforts of our enemies. Prizes are taken in no small numbers. A gentleman told me, a few days ago, that he had summed up the sugar which has been taken, and it amounted to three thousand hogsheads, since which two other ships have been taken and carried into Maryland. Thousands of schemes for privateering are afloat in American imaginations. Some are for taking the Hull ships, with woolens, for Amsterdam and Rotterdam; some are for the tin ships; some for the Irish linen ships; some for outward bound, and others for inward bound Indiamen; some for the Hudson's Bay ships, and many for West India sugar ships. Out of these speculations, many fruitless and some profitable projects will grow.

We have no news from New York. All is quiet as yet. Our expectations are raised. The eyes of the world are upon Washington and Howe, and their armies. The wishes and prayers of the virtuous part of it, I hope, will be answered. If not, yet virtues grow out of affliction. I repeat my request that you would ask some of the members of the General Court if they can send me horses; and if they cannot, that you would send them. I can live no longer without a servant and a horse.

42. John Adams

Philadelphia, 12 August 1776

MR. A. AND COLONEL WHIPPLE are at length gone. Colonel Tudor went off with them. They went away about three o'clock this afternoon. I wrote by A., and Colonel Whipple too; by the latter I sent two large bundles, which he promised to deliver to you. These middle States begin to taste the sweets of war. Ten thousand difficulties and wants occur, which they had no conception of before. Their militia are as clamorous, and impatient of discipline, and mutinous as ours, and more so. There has been seldom less than four thousand men in this city at a time, for a fortnight past, on their march to New Jersey. Here they wait, until we grow very angry about them, for canteens, camp kettles, blankets, tents, shoes, hose, arms, flints, and other dittoes, while we are under a very critical solicitude for our army at New York, on account of the insufficiency of men.

I want to be informed of the state of things with you; whether there is a scarcity of provisions of any kind, of West India articles, of clothing. Whether any trade is carried on, any fishery. Whether any vessels arrive from abroad, or whether any go to sea upon foreign voyages. I wish to know, likewise, what posture of defense you are in. What fortifications are at Nantasket, at Long Island, Pettick's Island, etc., and what men and officers there are to garrison them. We hear nothing from the Massachusetts, lately, in comparison of what we did when the army was before Boston.

I must not conclude without repeating my request that you would ask some of the members of the General Court to send me horses, and if they cannot, to send them yourself.

43. John Adams

Philadelphia, 14 August 1776

THIS IS THE anniversary of a memorable day in the history of America. A day when the principle of American resistance and independence was first asserted and carried into action. The stamp office fell before the rising spirit of our countrymen. It is not impossible that the two grateful brothers may make their grand attack this very day. If they should, it is possible it may be more glorious for this country than ever; it is certain it will become more memorable.

Your favors of August 1 and 5 came by yesterday's post. I congratulate you all upon your agreeable prospects. Even my pathetic little hero Charles, I hope will have the distemper finely. It is very odd that the Dr. can't put infection enough into his veins; nay, it is unaccountable to me that he has not taken it, in the natural way before now. I am under little apprehension, prepared as he is, if he should. I am concerned about you, much more. So many persons about you, sick. The children troublesome—your mind perplexed—yourself weak and relaxed. The situation must be disagreeable. The country air, and exercise, however, will refresh you.

I am put upon a committee to prepare a device for a golden medal, to commemorate the surrender of Boston to the American arms, and upon another to prepare devices for a great seal for the confederated States. There is a gentleman here of French extraction, whose name is Du Simitiere, a painter by profession, whose designs are very ingenious, and his drawings well executed. He has been applied to for his advice. I waited on him yesterday, and saw his sketches. For the medal he proposes, Liberty, with her spear and pileus, leaning on General Washington. The British fleet in Boston harbor with all their sterns towards the town, the American troops marching in. For the seal, he proposes the arms of the several nations from whence America has been peopled, as, English, Scotch, Irish, Dutch, German, etc., each in a shield. On one side of them, Liberty with her pileus, on the other, a rifler in his uniform, with his rifle-gun in one hand and his tomahawk in the other; this dress and these troops, with this kind of armor, being peculiar to America, unless the dress was known to the Romans. Dr. Franklin showed me yesterday a book containing an account of the dresses of all the Roman soldiers, one of which appeared exactly like it. This M. du Simitiere is a very curious man. He has begun a collection of materials for a history of this revolution. He begins with the first advices of the tea ships. He cuts out of the newspapers every scrap of intelligence and every piece of speculation, and pastes it upon clean paper, arranging them under the head of that State to which they belong, and intends to bind them up in volumes. He has a list of every speculation and pamphlet concerning independence, and another of those concerning forms of government.

Dr. F. proposes a device for a seal: Moses lifting up his wand and dividing the Red Sea, and Pharaoh in his chariot overwhelmed with the waters. This motto, "Rebellion to tyrants is obedience to God."

Mr. Jefferson proposed the children of Israel in the wilderness, led by a cloud by day and a pillar of fire by night; and on the other side, Hengist and Horsa, the Saxon chiefs from whom we claim the honor of being descended, and whose political principles and form of government we have assumed.

I proposed the choice of Hercules, as engraved by Gribelin, in some editions of Lord Shaftesbury's works. The hero resting on his club. Virtue pointing to her rugged mountain on one hand, and persuading him to ascend. Sloth, glancing at her flowery paths of pleasure, wantonly reclining on the ground, displaying the charms both of her eloquence and person, to seduce him into vice. But this is too complicated a group for a seal or medal, and it is not original.

I shall conclude by repeating my request for horses and a servant. Let the horses be good ones. I can't ride a bad horse so many hundred miles. If our affairs had not been in so critical a state at New York, I should have run away before now. But I am determined now to stay until some gentleman is sent here in my room, and until my horses come. But the time will be very tedious.

The whole force is arrived at Staten Island.

44. Abigail Adams

Boston, 14 August 1776

MR. SMITH CALLED upon me to-day and told me he should set out to-morrow for Philadelphia; desired I would write by him. I have shown him all the civility in my power, since he has been here, though not all I have wished to. I was much pleased with the account he gave us of the universal joy of his province upon the establishment of their new government, and the harmony subsisting between every branch of it. This State seems to behindhand of their neighbors. We want some master workman here. Those who are capable seem backward in this work, and some who are so tenacious of their own particular plan as to be loath to give it up. Some who are for abolishing both House and Council, affirming business was never so well done as in the provincial Congress, and they perhaps never so important.

Last Sunday, after service, the Declaration of Independence was read from the pulpit by order of Council. The Dr. concluded with asking a blessing "upon the United States of America even until the final restitution of all things."

Dr. Chauncy's address pleased me. The good man after having read it, lifted his eyes and hands to heaven. "God bless the United States of America, and let all the people say Amen."

One of his audience told me it universally struck them.

I have no news to write you. I am sure it will be none to tell you I am ever

Yours   PORTIA

45. Abigail Adams

14 August 1776

I WROTE YOU to-day by Mr. Smith but as I suppose this will reach you sooner, I omitted mentioning anything of my family in it. Nabby has enough of the small-pox for all the family beside. She is pretty well covered, not a spot but what is so sore that she can neither walk, sit, stand, or lay with any comfort. She is as patient as one can expect, but they are a very sore sort. If it was a disorder to which we should be subject more than once I would go as far as it was possible to avoid it. She is swelled a good deal. You will receive a particular account before this reaches you of the uncommon manner in which the small-pox acts; it baffles the skill of the most experienced here. Billy Cranch is now out with about forty, as so well as not to be detained at home for an hour for it. Charley remains in the same state he did.

Your letter of August 3 came by this day's post. I find it very convenient to be so handy. I can receive a letter at night, sit down and reply to it, and send it off in the morning.

You remark upon the deficiency of education in your countrymen. It never, I believe, was in a worse state, at least for many years. The college is not in the state one could wish. The scholars complain that their professor in philosophy is taken off by public business, to their great detriment. In this town I never saw so great a neglect of education. The poorer sort of children are wholly neglected, and left to range the streets, without schools, without business, given up to all evil. The town is not, as formerly, divided into wards. There is either too much business left upon the hands of a few, or too little care to do it. We daily see the necessity of a regular government.

You speak of our worthy brother. I often lament it, that a man so peculiarly formed for the education of youth, and so well qualified as he is in many branches of literature, excelling in philosophy and the mathematics, should not be employed in some public station. I know not the person who would make half so good a successor to Dr. Winthrop. He has a peculiar, easy manner of communicating his ideas to youth; and the goodness of his heart and the purity of his morals, without an affected austerity, must have a happy effect upon the minds of pupils.

If you complain of neglect of education in sons, what shall I say with regard to daughters, who every day experience the want of it? With regard to the education of my own children, I find myself soon out of my depth, destitute and deficient in every part of education.

I most sincerely wish that some more liberal plan might be laid and executed for the benefit of the rising generation, and that our new Constitution may be distinguished for encouraging learning and virtue. If we mean to have heroes, statesmen, and philosophers, we should have learned women. The world perhaps would laugh at me and accuse me of vanity, but you, I know, have a mind too enlarged and liberal to disregard the sentiment. If much depends, as is allowed, upon the early education of youth, and the first principles which are instilled take the deepest root, great benefit must arise from literary accomplishments in women.

Excuse me. My pen has run away with me. I have no thoughts of coming to Philadelphia. The length of time I have and shall be detained here would have prevented me, even if you had no thoughts of returning till December; but I live in daily expectation of seeing you here. Your health, I think, requires your immediate return. I expected Mr. Gerry would have set off before now, but he perhaps finds it very hard to leave his mistress. I won't say harder than some do to leave their wives. Mr. Gerry stood very high in my esteem. What is meat for one is not for another. No accounting for fancy. She is a queer dame and leads people wild dances.

But hush! Post, don't betray your trust and lose my letter. Nabby is poorly this morning. The pocks are near the turn, six or seven hundred boils are no agreeable feeling. You and I know not what a feeling it is. Miss Katy can tell. I had but three; they were very clever and filled nicely. The town instead of being clear of this distemper are now in the height of it, hundreds having it in the natural way through the deceitfulness of inoculation. Adieu ever yours. Breakfast waits.   PORTIA

46. John Adams

18 August 1776

MY LETTERS TO you are an odd mixture. They would appear to a stranger like the dish which is sometimes called *omnium gatherum*. This is the first time, I believe, that these two words were ever put together in writing. The literal interpretation I take to be "a collection of all things." But, as I said before, the words having never before been written, it is not possible to be very learned in telling you what the Arabic, Syriac, Chaldaic, Greek, and Roman commentators say upon the subject. Amidst all the rubbish that constitutes the heap, you will see a proportion of affection for my friends, my family, and country, that gives a complexion to the whole. I have a very tender, feeling heart. This country knows not, and never can know, the torments I have endured for its sake. I am glad it never can know, for it would give more pain to the benevolent and humane than I could wish even the wicked and malicious to feel.

I have seen in this world but a little of that pure flame of patriotism which certainly burns in some breasts. There is much of the ostentation and affectation of it. I have known a few who could not bear to entertain a selfish design, nor to be suspected by others of such a meanness; but these are not the most respected by the world. A man must be selfish, even to acquire great popularity. He must grasp for himself, under specious pretenses for the public good, and he must attach himself to his relations, connections, and friends, by becoming a champion for their interests, in order to form a phalanx about him for his own defense, to make them trumpeters of his praise, and sticklers for his fame, fortune, and honor.

My friend Warren, the late Governor Ward, and Mr. Gadsden are three characters in which I have seen the most generous disdain of every spice and species of such meanness. The two last had not great abilities, but they had pure hearts. Yet they had less influence than many others, who had neither so considerable parts nor any share at all of their purity of intention. Warren has both talents and virtues beyond most men in this world, yet his character has never been in proportion. Thus it always is and has been and will be. Nothing has ever given me more mortification than a suspicion that has been propagated of me, that I am actuated by private views and have been aiming at high places. The office of Chief Justice has occasioned this jealousy, and it never will be allayed until I resign it. Let me have my farm, family, and goosequill, and all the honors and offices this world has to bestow may go to those who deserve them better and desire them more. I covet them not. There are very few people in this world with whom I can bear to converse. I can treat all with decency and civility, and converse with them, when it is necessary, on points of business. But I am never happy in their company. This has made me a recluse and will one day make me a hermit. I had rather build stone wall upon Penn's Hill, than to be the first Prince in Europe, or the first General or first Senator in America.

Our expectations are very high of some great affair at New York.

47. John Adams

YESTERDAY MORNING I took a walk into Arch Street to see Mr. Peale's painter's room. Peale is from Maryland, a tender, soft, affectionate creature. He showed me a large picture containing a group of figures, which, upon inquiry, I found were his family: his mother and his wife's mother, himself and his wife, his brothers and sisters, and his children, sons and daughters, all young. There was a pleasant, a happy cheerfulness in their countenances, and a familiarity in their air towards each other.

He showed me one moving picture. His wife, all bathed in tears, with a child about six months old laid out upon her lap. This picture struck me prodigiously. He has a variety of portraits, very well done, but not so well as Copley's portraits. Copley is the greatest master that ever was in America. His portraits far exceed West's. Peale has taken General Washington, Dr. Franklin, Mrs. Washington, Mrs. Rush, Mrs. Hopkinson, Mr. Blair McClenachan and his little daughter in one picture, his lady and her little son in another. Peale showed me some books upon the art of painting. Among the rest one by Sir Joshua Reynolds, the President of the English Academy of Painters, by whom the pictures of General Conway and Colonel Barré, in Faneuil Hall, were taken. He showed me, too, a great number of miniature pictures. Among the rest, Mr. Hancock and his lady, Mr. Smith, of South Carolina, whom you saw the other day in Boston, Mr. Custis, and many others.

He showed me, likewise, draughts, or rather sketches, of gentlemen's seats in Virginia, where he had been, Mr. Corbin's, Mr. Page's, General Washington's, etc. Also a variety of rough drawings made by great masters in Italy, which he keeps as models. He showed me several imitations of heads, which he had made in clay, as large as the life, with his hands only. Among the rest, one of his own head and face, which was a great likeness. He is ingenious. He has vanity, loves finery, wears a sword, gold lace, speaks French, is capable of friendship, and strong family attachments and natural affections.

At this shop I met Mr. Francis Hopkinson, late a Mandamus Counsellor of New Jersey, now a member of the Continental Congress, who, it seems, is a native of Philadelphia, a son of a prothonotary of this county, who was a person much respected. The son was liberally educated, and is a painter and a poet. I have a curiosity to penetrate a little deeper into the bosom of this curious gentleman, and may possibly give you some more particulars concerning him. He is one of your pretty, little, curious, ingenious men. His head is not bigger than a large apple, less than our friend Pemberton, or Dr. Simon Tufts. I have not met with anything in natural history more amusing and entertaining than his personal appearance; yet he is genteel and well bred, and is very social.

I wish I had leisure and tranquillity of mind to amuse myself with those elegant and ingenious arts of painting, sculpture, statuary, architecture, and music. But I have not. A taste in all of them is an agreeable accomplishment. Mr. Hopkinson has taken in crayons with his own hand a picture of Miss Keys, a famous New Jersey beauty. He talks of bringing it to town, and in that case, I shall see it, I hope.

48. John Adams

Philadelphia, 25 August 1776

THE DAY BEFORE yesterday, and yesterday, we expected letters and papers by the post, but by some accident or mismanagement of the riders no post is arrived yet which has been a great disappointment to me. I watch with longing eyes for the post, because you have been very good, of late, in writing by every one. I long to hear that Charles is in as fair a way through the distemper as the rest of you.

Poor Barrell is violently ill, in the next chamber to mine, of an inflammatory fever. I hear every cough, sigh, and groan. His fate hangs in a critical suspense. The least thing may turn the scale against him. Miss Quincy is here, very humanely employed in nursing him. This goodness does her honor. Mr. Paine has recovered of his illness, and, by present appearances, is in better health than before. I hope it will not be my fate to be sick here. Indeed, I am not much afraid of these acute disorders: mine are more chronical, nervous, and slow. I must have a ride. I cannot make it do without it.

We are now approaching rapidly to the autumnal equinox, and no great blow has yet been struck, in the martial way, by our enemies, nor by us. If we should be blessed, this year, with a few storms as happy as those which fell out last year in the beginning of September, they will do much for us. The British fleet, where they now lie, have not a harbor so convenient or safe as they had last year. Another winter will do much for us too. We shall have more and better soldiers. We shall be better armed. We shall have a greater force at sea. We shall have more trade. Our artillery will be greatly increased, our officers will have more experience and our soldiers more discipline, our politicians more courage and confidence, and our enemies less hope. Our American commonwealths will be all completely formed and organized, and everything, I hope, will go on with greater vigor.

After I had written thus far, the post came in and brought me your favor of the 14th of August. Nabby by this time, I conclude, is well, and Charles, I hope, is broken out. Don't you recollect, upon this occasion, Dr. Byles's benediction to me when I was inoculated? As you will see the piquancy of it now, more than ever you could before, I will tell the story.

After having been ten or eleven days inoculated, I lay lolling on my bed in Major Cunningham's chamber, under the tree of liberty, with half a dozen young fellows as lazy as myself, all waiting and wishing for symptoms and eruptions; all of a sudden appeared at the chamber door the reverend Doctor with his rosy face, many-curled wig, and pontifical air and gait. "I have been thinking," says he, "that the clergy of this town ought, upon this occasion, to adopt the benediction of the Romish clergy, and, when we enter the apartment of the sick, to say in the foreign pronunciation, '*Pax tecum*.'" These words are spoken by foreigners, as the Dr. pronounced them, *Pox take 'em*. One would think Sir Isaac Newton's discovery of the system of gravitation did not require a deeper reach of thought than this frivolous pun.

Your plan of making our worthy brother, professor, would be very agreeable to me.

Your sentiments of the importance of education in women are exactly agreeable to my own. Yet the *femmes savantes* are contemptible characters. So is that of a pedant universally, how muchsoever of a male he may be. In reading history, you will generally observe, when you light upon a great character, whether a general, a statesman, or philosopher, some female about him, either in the character of a mother, wife, or sister, who has knowledge and ambition above the ordinary level of women, and that much of his eminence is owing to her precepts, example, or instigation, in some shape or other. Let me mention an example or two. Sempronius Gracchus and Caius Gracchus, two great though unfortunate men, are said to have been instigated to their great actions by their mother, who, in order to stimulate their ambition, told them that she was known in Rome by the title of the mother-in-law of Scipio, not the mother of the Gracchi. Thus she excited their emulation and put them upon reviving the old project of an equal division of the conquered lands (a genuine republican measure, though it had been too long neglected to be then practicable), in order to make their names as illustrious as Scipio's. The great Duke who first excited the Portuguese to revolt from the Spanish monarchy was spurred on to his great enterprise by a most artful and ambitious wife, and thus indeed you will find it very generally. What tale have you heard of Gerry? What mistress is he courting?

49. Abigail Adams

Boston, 25 August 1776

I SENT JOHNNY last evening to the post-office for letters. He soon
returned, and pulling one from under his gown gave it me. The
young rogue, smiling and watching mamma's countenance, draws
out another and then another, highly gratified to think he had so
many presents to bestow.

Our friends are very kind. My father sends his horse, and
Dr. Tufts has offered me another one he had of uncle Quincy, about
five years old. He has never been on journeys, but is able enough.
Mr. Bass is just come, and says he cannot set out till tomorrow week
without great damage to his business. He has been a long time out
of stock, and about a week ago obtained a quantity and has engaged
twenty pair of shoes which will be equal to twenty dollars to him,
which he must lose if I will not consent to his tarrying till then.
Though I urged him to set out to-morrow, yet the horses will be
in a better state, as they will not be used, and more able to perform
the journey. I am obliged to consent to his tarrying till then, when
you may certainly expect him.

Bass is afraid that the Dr.'s horse will not be able to travel so fast
as he must go. He will go and see him, and in case he is not, your
brother has promised to let one of his go. I only have to regret that
I did not sooner make trial of my friends, and have sent for you
three weeks ago. I fear you will think me negligent, and inattentive.
If I had been at home, I should have been sooner in a capacity to
have assisted you. I was talking of sending for you and trying to
procure horses for you when little Charles, who lay upon the couch
covered over with small-pox, and nobody knew that he heard or

regarded anything which was said, lifted up his head and says, "Mamma, take my dollar and get a horse for papa." Poor fellow has had a tedious time of it as well as I, but 'tis now upon the turn, and he is much easier and better. I hope I shall be able to get out of town a Saturday next.

Mr. and Mrs. Cranch with their children went out a Friday. I feel rather lonely. Such a change from one or two and twenty to only five or six is a great alteration.

I took the liberty of sending my compliments to General Lincoln, and asking him some questions which you proposed to me, but which I was totally unable to answer, and he has promised a particular reply to them.

As to provisions, there is no scarcity. 'Tis true they are high, but that is more owing to the advanced price of labor than the scarcity. English goods of every kind are not purchasable, at least by me. They are extravagantly high. West India goods articles are very high, all except sugars, which have fallen half since I came into town. Our New England rum is four shillings per gallon; molasses the same price; loaf sugar two and fourpence; cotton-wool four shillings per pound; sheep's wool two shillings; flax one and sixpence. In short, one hundred pounds two years ago would purchase more than two will now.

House rent in this town is very low. Some of the best and genteelest houses rent for twenty pounds a year. Ben Hallowell's has been offered for ten, and Mr. Chardon's for thirteen pounds six shillings and eight pence.

The privateer *Independence,* which sailed from Plymouth about three weeks ago, has taken a Jamaica-man laden with sugars, and sent her into Marblehead last Saturday. I hear the *Defence* has taken another. I think we make a fine hand at prizes.

Colonel Quincy desires me to ask you whether you have received a letter from him; he wrote you some time ago.

I like Dr. Franklin's device for a seal. It is such a one as will please most, at least it will be most agreeable to the spirit of New England.

We have not any news here—anxiously waiting the event, and in daily expectation of hearing tidings from New York. Heaven grant they may be glorious for our country and countrymen. Then will I glory in being an American.

Ever, Ever yours,   PORTIA

P.S. We are in such want of lead as to be obliged to take down the leads from the windows in this town.

50. Abigail Adams

Boston, 29 August 1776

I HAVE SPENT the three days past almost entirely with you. The weather has been stormy. I have had little company, and I have amused myself in my closet, reading over the letters I have received from you since I have been here.

I have possession of my aunt's chamber, in which, you know, is a very convenient, pretty closet, with a window which looks into her flower garden. In this closet are a number of bookshelves, which are but poorly furnished. However I have a pretty little desk or cabinet here, where I write all my letters and keep my papers, unmolested by any one. I do not covet my neighbor's goods, but I should like to be the owner of such conveniences. I always had a fancy for a closet with a window, which I could more particularly call my own.

Here I say I have amused myself in reading and thinking of my absent friend, sometimes with a mixture of pain, sometimes with pleasure, sometimes anticipating a joyful and happy meeting, whilst my heart would bound and palpitate with the pleasing idea, and with the purest affection I have held you to my bosom till my whole soul has dissolved in tenderness and my pen fallen from my hand. How often do I reflect with pleasure that I hold in possession a heart equally warm with my own, and full as susceptable of the tenderest impressions, and who even now whilst he is reading here, feels all I describe. Forgive this reverie, this delusion, and since I am debarred real, suffer me to enjoy and indulge in ideal pleasures— and tell me they are not inconsistent with the stern virtue of a senator and a patriot. I must leave my pen to recover myself and write in another strain.

I feel anxious for a post day, and am full as solicitous for two letters a week, and as uneasy if I do not get them, as I used to be when I got but one in a month or five weeks. Thus do I presume upon indulgence, and this is human nature. It brings to my mind a sentiment of one of your correspondents, to wit, that "man is the only animal who is hungry with his belly full."

Last evening Dr. Cooper came in and brought me your favor, from the post-office, of August 18 and Colonel Whipple arrived yesterday morning and delivered to me the two bundles you sent and a letter of the 12th of August. They have already afforded me much amusement, and I expect much more from them.

I am sorry to find from your last, as well as from some others of your letters, that you feel so dissatisfied with the office to which you are chosen. Though in your acceptance of it I know you were actuated by the purest motives, and I know of no person here so well qualified to discharge the important duties of it, yet I will not urge you to it. In accepting of it you must be excluded from all other employments. There never will be a salary adequate to the importance of the office or to support you and your family from penury. If you possessed a fortune I would urge you to it, in spite of all the fleers and gibes of minds which themselves are incapable of acting a disinterested part, and have no conception that others can. I have never heard any one speak about it, nor did I know that such insinuations had been thrown out.

Pure and disinterested virtue must ever be its own reward. Mankind are too selfish and too depraved to discern the pure gold from the baser metal.

I wish for peace and tranquillity. All my desire and all my ambition is to be esteemed and loved by my partner, to join with him in the education and instruction of our little ones, to sit under our own vines in peace, liberty, and safety.

Adieu, my dearest friend! Soon, soon return to your most affectionate   PORTIA

P.S. Charley is cleverly. A very odd report has been propagated in Braintree, namely, that you were poisoned upon your return, at New York.

51. John Adams

Philadelphia, 5 September 1776

MR. BASS ARRIVED this day with the joyful news that you were all well. By this opportunity I shall send you a canister of green tea by Mr. Hare. Before Mr. Gerry went away from hence, I asked Mrs. Yard to send a pound of green tea to you. She readily agreed. When I came home at night I was told Mr. G. was gone. I asked Mrs. Y. if she had sent the canister. She said, yes, and that Mr. G. undertook to deliver it with a great deal of pleasure. From that time I flattered myself you would have the poor relief of a dish of good tea, under all your fatigues with the children, and under all the disagreeable circumstances attending the small-pox, and I never conceived a single doubt that you had received it, until Mr. Gerry's return. I asked him, accidentally, whether he delivered it, and he said, "Yes, to Mr. Samuel Adams's lady." I was astonished. He misunderstood Mrs. Yard entirely; for upon inquiry she affirms she told him it was for Mrs. J. A. I was so vexed at this that I have ordered another canister, and Mr. Hare has been kind enough to undertake to deliver it. How the dispute will be settled I don't know. You must send a card to Mrs. S. A., and let her know that the canister was intended for you, and she may send it you, if she chooses, as it was charged to me. It is amazingly dear; nothing less than forty shillings, lawful money, a pound.

I am rejoiced that my horses are come. I shall now be able to take a ride. But it is uncertain when I shall set off for home. I will not go at present. Affairs are too delicate and critical. The panic may seize whom it will. It shall not seize me. I will stay here until the public countenance is better, or much worse. It must and will be better. I think it is not now bad. Lies by the million will be told you. Don't believe any of them. There is no danger of the communication being cut off between the northern and southern colonies. I can go home when I please, in spite of all the fleet and army of Great Britain.

52. John Adams

Philadelphia, Friday, 6 September 1776

THIS DAY, I think, has been the most remarkable of all. Sullivan came here from Lord Howe, five days ago, with a message that his lordship desired a half an hour's conversation with some of the members of Congress in their private capacities. We have spent three or four days in debating whether we should take any notice of it. I have, to the utmost of my abilities, during the whole time, opposed our taking any notice of it. But at last it was determined by a majority, "that the Congress being the representatives of the free and independent States of America, it was improper to appoint any of their members to confer in their private characters with his lordship. But they would appoint a committee of their body to wait on him, to know whether he had power to treat with Congress upon terms of peace, and to hear any propositions that his lordship may think proper to make."

When the committee came to be balloted for, Dr. Franklin and your humble servant were unanimously chosen. Colonel R. H. Lee and Mr. Rutledge and an equal number; but, upon a second vote, Mr. Rutledge was chosen. I requested to be excused, but was desired to consider of it until to-morrow. My friends here advise me to go. All the stanch and intrepid are very earnest with me to go, and the timid and wavering, if any such there are, agree in the request. So I believe I shall undertake the journey. I doubt whether his lordship will see us, but the same committee will be directed to inquire into the state of the army at New York, so that there will be business enough, if his lordship makes none. It would fill this letter-book to give you all the arguments for and against this measure, if I had liberty to attempt it. His lordship seems to have been playing off a number

115

of Machiavelian manoeuvres, in order to throw upon us the odium of continuing this war. Those who have been advocates for the appointment of this committee are for opposing manoeuvre to manoeuvre, and are confident that the consequence will be that the odium will fall upon him. However this may be, my lesson is plain, to ask a few questions and take his answers.

I can think of but one reason for their putting me upon this embassy, and that is this. An idea has crept into many minds here that his lordship is such another as Mr. Hutchinson, and they may possibly think that a man who has been accustomed to penetrate into the mazy windings of Hutchinson's heart, and the serpentine wiles of his head, may be tolerably qualified to converse with his lordship.

Sunday, 8 September

Yesterday's post brought me yours of August 29. The report you mention, "that I was poisoned upon my return home, at New York," I suppose will be thought to be a prophecy delivered by the oracle, in mystic language, and meant that I should be politically or morally poisoned by Lord Howe. But the prophecy shall be false.

53. Abigail Adams

Braintree, 7 September 1776

LAST MONDAY I left the town of Boston, underwent the operation of a smoking at the lines, and arrived at my brother Cranch's, where we go for purification; there I tarried till Wednesday, and then came home, which seemed greatly endeared to me by my long absence. I think I never felt greater pleasure at coming home after an absence in my life. Yet I felt a vacuum in my breast and sent a sigh to Philadelphia. I longed for a dear friend to rejoice with me. Charley is banished yet. I keep him at his aunt Cranch's, out of the way of those who have not had the distemper; his arm has many scabs upon it, which are yet very sore. He is very weak and sweats a-nights prodigiously. I am now giving him the bark. He recovered very fast considering how ill he was. I pity your anxiety and feel sorry that I wrote you when he was so bad, but I knew not how it might turn with him; had it been otherwise than well, it might have proved a greater shock than to have known that he was ill.

This night our good uncle came from town and brought yours of August 20, 21, 25, 27, and 28, for all of which I most sincerely thank you. I have felt uneasy to hear from you. The report of your being dead has no doubt reached you by Bass, who heard enough of it before he came away. It took its rise among the Tories, who, as Swift said of himself, "By their fears betray their hopes." How they should ever take it into their heads that you was poisoned at New York, a fortnight before that we heard anything of that villain Zedtwitz's plan of poisoning the waters of the city, I cannot tell. I am sometimes ready to suspect that there is a communication between the Tories of every State; for they seem to know all news that is passing before it is known by the Whigs.

We have had many stories concerning engagements upon Long Island this week; of our lines being forced and of our troops returning to New York. Particulars we have not yet obtained. All we can learn is that we have been unsuccessful there; having lost many men as prisoners, among whom are Lord Stirling and General Sullivan.

But if we should be defeated, I think we shall not be conquered. A people fired like the Romans with love of their country and of liberty, a zeal for the public good, and a noble emulation of glory, will not be disheartened or dispirited by a succession of unfortunate events. But like them may we learn by defeat the power of becoming invincible!

I hope to hear from you by every post till you return. The herbs you mention I never received. I was upon a visit to Mrs. S. Adams about a week after Mr. Gerry returned, when she entertained me with a very fine dish of green tea. The scarcity of the article made me ask her where she got it. She replied that her *sweetheart* sent it to her by Mr. Gerry. I said nothing, but thought my sweetheart might have been equally kind, considering the disease I was visited with, and that was recommended a bracer. A little after, you mentioned a couple of bundles sent. I supposed one of them might contain the article, but found they were letters. How Mr. Gerry should make such a mistake I know not. I shall take the liberty of sending for what is left of it, though I suppose it is half gone, as it was very freely used. If you had mentioned a single word of it in your letter, I should have immediately found out the mistake.

It is said that the efforts of our enemies will be to stop the communication between the Colonies by taking possession of Hudson's Bay. Can it be effected? The *Milford* frigate rides triumphant in our bay, taking vessels every day, and no colony or Continental vessel has yet attempted to hinder her. She mounts but twenty-eight guns, but is one of the finest sailers in the British navy. They complain we have not weighty metal enough, and I suppose truly. The rage for privateering is as great here as anywhere, and I believe the success has been as great.

It will not be in my power to write you so regularly as when I was in town. I shall not fail doing it once a week. If you come home by the post road you must inquire for letters wherever the post set out from. 'Tis here a very general time of health. I think 'tis near a twelvemonth since the pestilence raged here. I fear your being seized with a fever; 'tis very prevalent I hear where you are. I pray God preserve you and return you in health. The Court will not accept your resignation; they will appoint Mr. Dalton and Mr. Dana to relieve you. I am most affectionately yours.

54. John Adams

Philadelphia, Saturday, 14 September 1776

YESTERDAY MORNING I returned with Dr. Franklin and Mr. Rutledge from Staten Island, where we met Lord Howe and had about three hours' conversation with him. The result of this interview will do no disservice to us. It is now plain that his lordship has no power but what is given him in the act of Parliament. His commission authorizes him to grant pardons upon submission, and to converse, confer, consult, and advise with such persons as he may think proper, upon American grievances, upon the instructions to Governors and the acts of Parliament, and if any errors should be found to have crept in, his Majesty and the ministry were willing they should be rectified.

I found yours of 31st of August and 2d of September. I now congratulate you on your return home with the children. I am sorry to find you anxious on account of idle reports. Don't regard them. I think our friends are to blame to mention such silly stories. What good do they expect to do by it?

My ride has been of service to me. We were absent but four days. It was an agreeable excursion. His lordship is about fifty years of age. He is a well-bred man, but his address is not so irresistible as it has been represented. I could name you many Americans, in your own neighborhood, whose art, address, and abilities are greatly superior. His head is rather confused, I think.

When I shall return I can't say. I expect now every day fresh hands from Watertown.

55. Abigail Adams

15 September 1776

I HAVE BEEN so much engaged with company this week, that though I never cease to think of you I have not had leisure to write. It has been High Court week with us. Judge Cushing and lady kept here. The judges all dined with me one day and the bar another day. The Court sit till Saturday night and then are obliged to continue many causes. The people seem to be pleased and gratified at seeing justice returning into its old regular channel again.

I this week received two letters, one dated 27th and one 29th July. Where they have been these two months I cannot conceive. I hear of another by the express, but have not yet been able to find it. I write now not knowing where to direct to you; whether you are in the American Senate or on board the British fleet, is a matter of uncertainty. I hear to-day that you are one of a committee sent by Congress to hold a conference with Lord Howe. Some say to negotiate an exchange of General Sullivan. Others say you are charged with other matters.

May you be as wise as serpents. I wish to hear from you. The 28th of August was the last date. I may have letters at the post-office. The town is not yet clear of the small-pox, which makes it difficult for me to get a conveyance from there unless I send on purpose.

I only write now to let you know we are all well, anxiously longing for your return.

As this is a child of chance I do not choose to say anything more than that I am   Sincerely Yours.

56. Abigail Adams

I SIT DOWN this evening to write you, but I hardly know what to think about your going to New York. The story has been told so many times, and with circumstances so particular, that I with others have given some heed to it, though my not hearing anything of it from you leaves me at a loss.

Yours of September 4 came to hand last night. Our worthy uncle is a constant attendant upon the post-office for me, and brought it me. Yours of September 5 came to-night to Braintree, and was left as directed with the canister. I am sorry you gave yourself so much trouble about it. I got about half you sent me by Mr. Gerry. Am much obliged to you, and hope to have the pleasure of making the greater part of it for you. Your letter damped my spirits. When I had no expectation of your return till December, I endeavored to bring my mind to acquiesce in the too painful situation. I have reckoned the days since Bass went away a hundred times over, and every letter expected to find the day set for your return.

But now I fear it is far distant. I have frequently been told that the communication would be cut off, and that you would not be able ever to return. Sometimes I have been told so by those who really wished it might be so, with malicious pleasure. Sometimes your timid folks have apprehended that it would be so. I wish anything would bring you nearer. If there is really any danger I should think you would remove. It is a plan your enemies would rejoice to see accomplished, and will effect if it lies in their power. I am not apt to be intimidated, you know. I have given as little heed to that, and a thousand other bugbear reports, as possible.

I have slept as soundly since my return, notwithstanding all the ghosts and hobgoblins, as ever I did in my life. It is true I never close my eyes at night till I have been to Philadelphia, and my first visit in the morning is there.

How unfeeling are the world! They tell me they heard you was dead with as little sensibility as a stock or a stone; and I have now got to be provoked at it, and can hardly help snubbing the person who tells me so.

The story of your being upon this conference at New York came in a letter, as I am told, from R. T. P. to his brother-in-law G——fe. Many, very many have been the conjectures of the multitude upon it. Some have supposed the war concluded, the nation settled. Others an exchange of prisoners. Others, a reconciliation with Britain, etc., etc.

I cannot consent to your tarrying much longer. I know your health must greatly suffer from so constant application to business, and so little exercise. Besides, I shall send you word by and by, as Regulus's steward did, that whilst you are engaged in the Senate, your own domestic affairs require your presence at home; and that your wife and children are in danger of wanting bread. If the Senate of America will take care of us, as the Senate of Rome did of the family of Regulus, you may serve them again; but unless you return, what little property you possess will be lost. In the first place the house at Boston is going to ruin. When I was there, I hired a girl to clean it; it had a cart load of dirt in it. I speak within bounds. One of the chambers was used to keep poultry in, another sea coal, and another salt. You may conceive how it looked. The house is so exceedingly damp, being shut up, that the floors are mildewed, the ceiling falling down, and the paper mouldy and falling from the walls. I took care to have it opened and aired whilst I tarried in town. I put it into the best state I could.

In the next place, the lighter of which you are, or should be, part owner is lying rotting at the wharf. One year more without any care, and she is worth nothing. You have no bill of sale, no right to convey any part of her should any person appear to purchase her. The pew I let, after having paid a tax for the repairs of the meeting-house.

As to what is here under my more immediate inspection, I do the best I can with it. But it will not, at the high price labor is, pay its way. I know the weight of public cares lie so heavy upon you that I have been loath to mention your own private ones.

The best accounts we can collect from New York, assure us that our men fought valiantly. We are no wise dispirited here. We possess a spirit that will not be conquered. If our men are all drawn off and we should be attacked, you would find a race of Amazons in America. But I trust we shall yet tread down our enemies.

I must entreat you to remember me often. I never think your letters half long enough. I do not complain. I have no reason to. No one can boast of more letters than your   PORTIA

57. John Adams

Philadelphia, 22 September 1776

WE HAVE AT last agreed upon a plan for forming a regular army. We have offered twenty dollars and a hundred acres of land to every man who will enlist during the war. And a new set of articles of war are agreed on. I will send you, if I can, a copy of these resolutions and regulations.

I am at a loss what to write. News we have not. Congress seems to be forgotten by the armies. We are most unfaithfully served in the post-office, as well as many other offices, civil and military. Unfaithfulness in public stations is deeply criminal. But there is no encouragement to be faithful. Neither profit, nor honor, nor applause is acquired by faithfulness. But I know by what. There is too much corruption even in this infant age of our republic. Virtue is not in fashion. Vice is not infamous.

1 October 1776

Since I wrote the foregoing, I have not been able to find time to write you a line. Although I cannot write you so often as I wish, you are never out of my thoughts. I am repining at my hard lot in being torn from you much oftener than I ought. I have often mentioned to you the multiplicity of my engagements, and have been once exposed to the ridicule and censure of the world for mentioning the great importance of the business which lay upon me; and if this letter should ever see the light, it would be again imputed to vanity that I mention to you how busy I am. But I must repeat it by way of apology for not writing you oftener. From four o'clock in the morning until ten at night, I have not a single moment which I can call my own. I will not say that I expect to run distracted, to grow melancholy, to drop in an apoplexy, or fall into a consumption; but I do say, it is little less than a miracle that one or other of these misfortunes has not befallen me before now.

Your favors of 15th, 20th, and 23d September are now before me. Every line from you gives me inexpressible pleasure, but it is a great grief to me that I can write no oftener to you. There is one thing which excites my utmost indignation and contempt. I mean the brutality with which people talk to you of my death. I beg you would openly affront every man, woman, or child, for the future, who mentions any such thing to you, except your relations and friends, whose affections you cannot doubt. I expect it of all my friends, that they resent, as affronts to me, every repetition of such reports.

I shall inclose to you Governor Livingston's speech; the most elegant and masterly ever made in America. Depend upon it, the enemy cannot cut off the communication. I can come home when I will. They have New York, and this is their *ne plus ultra*.

58. Abigail Adams

29 September 1776

NOT SINCE THE 6th of September have I had one line from you, which makes me very uneasy. Are you all this time conferring with his Lordship? Is there no communication? or are the post-riders all dismissed? Let the cause be what it will, not hearing from you has given me much uneasiness.

We seem to be kept in total ignorance of affairs at York. I hope you at Congress are more enlightened. Who fell, who are wounded, who prisoners, or their number, is as undetermined as it was the day after the battle. If our army is in ever so critical a state I wish to know it, and the worst of it. If all America is to be ruined and undone by a pack of cowards and knaves, I wish to know it. Pitiable is the lot of their commander. Caesar's tenth legion never was forgiven. We are told for truth that a regiment of Yorkers refused to quit the city, and that another regiment behaved like a pack of cowardly villains by quitting their posts. If they are unjustly censured, it is for want of proper intelligence.

I am sorry to see a spirit so venal prevailing everywhere. When our men were drawn out for Canada, a very large bounty was given them; and now another call is made upon us; no one will go without a large bounty, though only for two months, and each town seems to think its honor engaged in outbidding one another. The province pay is forty shillings. In addition to that, this town voted to make it up six pounds. They then drew out the persons most unlikely to go, and they are obliged to give three pounds to hire a man. Some pay the whole fine, ten pounds. Forty men are now drafted from this town. More than one half, from sixteen to fifty, are now in the service. This method of conducting will create a general uneasiness in the Continental army. I hardly think you can be sensible how much we are thinned in this province.

The rage for privateering is as great here as anywhere. Vast numbers are employed in that way. If it is necessary to make any more drafts upon us, the women must reap the harvests. I am willing to do my part. I believe I could gather corn, and husk it; but I should make a poor figure at digging potatoes.

There has been a report that a fleet was seen in our bay yesterday. I cannot conceive from whence, nor do I believe the story.

'Tis said you have been upon Staten Island to hold your conference. 'Tis a little odd that I have never received the least intimation of it from you. Did you think I should be alarmed? Don't you know me better than to think me a coward? I hope you will write me everything concerning this affair. I have a great curiosity to know the result.

As to government, nothing is yet done about it. The Church is opened here every Sunday, and the King prayed for, as usual, in open defiance of Congress. Parker of Boston is more discreet and so is Serjeant.

You have wrote me once or twice to know whether your brother inclined to go into the service. I think he wholly declines it. As to mine I have not heard anything from him since his application to Court. Nathaniel Belcher goes as captain and Tertius Bass as lieutenant from this town. They march tomorrow. Poor Soper, we have lost him with a nervous fever; he died a Friday. A great loss to this town, a man so enterprising a temper, more especially when we are so destitute of them. I should be obliged to you if you would direct Bass to buy me a Barcelona handkerchief and two ounces of thread number eighteen. Mr. Gerry said goods were five percent dearer here than with you, and by the way I hope you are not charged equally dear for the last canister as for the first; the first is the best of Hyson, the other very good Souchong.

If the next post does not bring me a letter, I think I will leave off writing, for I shall not believe you get mine.

Adieu.   Yours,

P.S. Master John has become post-rider from Boston to Braintree.

59. John Adams

Philadelphia, 4 October 1776

I AM SEATED in a large library room with eight gentlemen round about me, all engaged in conversation. Amidst these interruptions, how shall I make it out to write a letter?

The first day of October, the day appointed by the charter of Pennsylvania for the annual election of Representatives, has passed away, and two counties only have chosen members, Bucks and Chester. The Assembly is therefore dead and the Convention is dissolved. A new Convention is to be chosen the beginning of November. The proceedings of the late Convention are not well liked by the best of the Whigs. Their Constitution is reprobated, and the oath with which they have endeavored to prop it, by obliging every man to swear that he will not add to, or diminish from, or any way alter that Constitution, before he can vote, is execrated.

We live in the age of political experiments. Among many that will fail, some, I hope, will succeed. But Pennsylvania will be divided and weakened, and rendered much less vigorous in the cause by the wretched ideas of government which prevail in the minds of many people in it.

60. John Adams

Philadelphia, 8 October 1776

I OUGHT TO acknowledge with gratitude your constant kindness in writing to me by every post. Your favor of 29 September came by the last. I wish it had been in my power to have returned your civilities with the same punctuality, but it has not. Long before this, you have received letters from me, and newspapers containing a full account of the negotiation. The communication is still open, and the post-riders now do their duty, and will continue to do so.

I assure you, we are as much at a loss about affairs at New York as you are. In general, our Generals were outgeneraled on Long Island, and Sullivan and Stirling with a thousand men were made prisoners, in consequence of which and several other unfortunate circumstances a council of war thought it prudent to retreat from that island and Governor's Island, and then from New York. They are now posted at Haarlem, about ten or eleven miles from the city. They left behind them some provisions, some cannon, and some baggage. Wherever the men of war have approached, our militia have most manfully turned their backs and run away, officers and men, like sturdy fellows; and their panics have sometimes seized the regular regiments. One little skirmish on Montresor's Island ended with the loss of the brave Major Henley and the disgrace of the rest of the party. Another skirmish, which might indeed be called an action, ended in the defeat and shameful flight of the enemy, with the loss of the brave Colonel Knowlton on our part. The enemy have possession of Paulus Hook and Bergen Point, places on the Jersey side of North River. By this time their force is so divided between Staten Island, Long Island, New York, Paulus Hook, and

Bergen Point, that I think they will do no great matter more this fall, unless the expiration of the term of enlistment of our army should disband it. If our new enlistment fill up for soldiers during the war, we shall do well enough. Everybody must encourage this.

You are told that a regiment of Yorkers behaved ill, and it may be true; but I can tell you that several regiments of Massachusetts men behaved ill too. The spirit of venality you mention is the most dreadful and alarming enemy America has to oppose. It is as rapacious and insatiable as the grave. We are in the *faece Romuli non republica Platonis*. This predominant avarice will ruin America, if she is ever ruined. If God Almighty does not interfere by his grace to control this universal idolatry to the mammon of unrighteousness, we shall be given up to the chastisements of his judgments. I am ashamed of the age I live in.

You surprise me with your account of the prayers in public for an abdicated king, a pretender to the crown. Nothing of that kind is heard in this place, or any other part of the continent but New York and the place you mention. This practice is treason against the State, and cannot be long tolerated.

I lament the loss of Soper, as an honest and useful member of society.

Don't leave off writing to me. I write as often as I can. I am glad master John has an office so useful to his mamma and papa as that of post-rider.

61. John Adams

Dedham, 9 January 1777

THE IRRESISTIBLE HOSPITALITY of Dr. Sprague and his lady has prevailed upon me and my worthy fellow-traveller to put up at his happy seat. We had an agreeable ride to this place, and to-morrow morning we set off for Providence, or some other route.

Present my affection in the tenderest manner to my little deserving daughter and my amiable sons. It was cruel parting this morning. My heart was most deeply affected, although I had the presence of mind to appear composed. May God Almighty's providence protect you, my dear, and all our little ones. My good genius, my guardian angel, whispers me that we shall see happier days, and that I shall live to enjoy the felicities of domestic life with her whom my heart esteems above all earthly blessings.

62. John Adams

Hartford, 13 January 1777

THE RIDING HAS been so hard and rough, and the weather so cold, that we have not been able to push farther than this place. My little colt has performed very well hitherto, and I think will carry me through this journey very pleasantly.

Our spirits have been cheered by two or three pieces of good news, which Commissary Trumbull, who is now with me, tells us he saw yesterday in a letter from General Washington, who has gained another considerable advantage of the enemy at Stony Brook, in the Jerseys, as General Putnam has gained another at Burlington, and the Jersey militia a third. The particulars you will have, before this reaches you, in the public prints. The communication of intelligence begins to be more open, and we have no apprehensions of danger in the route we shall take. Howe has reason to repent of his rashness, and will have more.

My love to my dear little ones. They are all very good children, and I have no doubt will continue so. I will drop a line as often as I can. Adieu.

63. John Adams

Hartford, 14 January 1777

IT IS NOW generally believed that General Washington has killed and taken at least two thousand of Mr. Howe's army since Christmas. Indeed, the evidence of it is from the General's own letters. You know I ever thought Mr. Howe's march through the Jerseys a rash step. It has proved so. But how much more so would it have been thought if the Americans could all have viewed it in that light and exerted themselves as they might and ought! The whole flock would infallibly have been taken in the net.

The little nest of hornets in Rhode Island! Is it to remain unmolested this winter? The honor of New England is concerned. If they are not ousted, I will never again glory in being a New England man. There are now New England Generals, officers, and soldiers, and if something is not done, any man may, after that, call New England men poltroons, with all my heart.

64. John Adams

Fishkill, 1777

AFTER A MARCH like that of Hannibal over the Alps, we arrived last night at this place, where we found the utmost difficulty to get forage for our horses and lodgings for ourselves, and at last were indebted to the hospitality of a private gentleman, Colonel Brinkhoff, who very kindly cared for us.

We came from Hartford through Farmington, Southington, Waterbury, Woodbury, New Milford, New Fairfield, the oblong, etc., to Fishkill. Of all the mountains I ever passed these are the worst. We found one advantage, however, in the cheapness of travelling. I don't find one half of the discontent nor of the terror here that I left in the Massachusetts. People seem sanguine that they shall do something grand this winter.

I am well and in good spirits. My horse performs extremely well. He clambers over mountains that my old mare would have stumbled on. The weather has been dreadfully severe.

65. John Adams

Poughkeepsie, 19 January 1777

THERE IS TOO much ice in Hudson's River to cross it in ferryboats, and too little to cross it without, in most places, which has given us the trouble of riding up the Albany road as far as this place, where we expect to go over on the ice; but if we should be disappointed here, we must go up as far as Esopus, about fifteen miles farther.

This, as well as Fishkill, is a pretty village. We are almost wholly among the Dutch, zealous against the Tories, who have not half the tranquillity here that they have in the town of Boston, after all the noise that has been made about New York Tories. We are treated with the utmost respect wherever we go, and have met with nothing like an insult from any person whatever. I heard ten reflections and twenty sighs and groans among my constituents to one here.

I shall never have done hoping that my countrymen will contrive some *coup de main* for the wretches at Newport. The winter is the time. Our enemies have divided their force. Let us take advantage of it.

66. John Adams

Bethlehem, Orange County,
State of New York, 20 January 1777

THIS MORNING WE crossed the North River, at Poughkeepsie, on the ice, after having ridden many miles on the east side of it, to find a proper place. We landed in New Marlborough, and passed through that and Newborough, to New Windsor, where we dined. This place is nearly opposite to Fishkill, and but little above the Highlands, where Fort Constitution and Fort Montgomery stand. The Highlands are a grand sight, a range of vast mountains which seem to be rolling like a tumbling sea. From New Windsor we came to this place, where we put up, and now we have a free and uninterrupted passage in a good road to Pennsylvania.

General Washington, with his little army, is at Morristown. Cornwallis, with his larger one, at Brunswick. Oh, that the Continental army was full! Now is the time!

My little horse holds out finely, although we have lost much time, and travelled a great deal of unnecessary way, to get over the North River. We have reports of our people's taking Fort Washington again, and taking four hundred more prisoners and six more pieces of cannon. But as I know not the persons who bring these accounts, I pay no attention to them.

67. John Adams

*Easton, at the Forks of Delaware River, in the
State of Pennsylvania, 24 January 1777*

WE HAVE AT last crossed the Delaware and are agreeably lodged at
Easton, a little town situated on a point of land formed by the Delaware
on one side, and the river Lehigh on the other. There is an elegant
stone Church here, built by the Dutch people, by whom the town
is chiefly inhabited, and what is remarkable, because uncommon,
the Lutherans and Calvinists united to build this Church, and the
Lutheran and Calvinist ministers alternately officiate in it. There is
also a handsome Court House. The buildings, public and private,
are all of limestone. Here are some Dutch Jews.

Yesterday we had the pleasure of seeing the Moravian mills in
New Jersey. These mills belong to the society of Moravians in
Bethlehem in Pennsylvania. They are a great curiosity. The building
is of limestone, four stories high. It is not in my power to give a
particular description of this piece of mechanism. A vast quantity of
grain of all sorts is collected here.

We have passed through the famous county of Sussex in New
Jersey, where the Sussex Court House stands, and where, we have
so often been told, the Tories are so numerous and dangerous.
We met with no molestation nor insult. We stopped at some of
the most noted Tory houses, and were treated everywhere with
the utmost respect. Upon the strictest inquiry I could make, I was
assured that a great majority of the inhabitants are stanch Whigs.
Sussex, they say, can take care of Sussex. And yet all agree that there
are more Tories in that county than in any other. If the British
army should get into that county in sufficient numbers to protect

the Tories, there is no doubt to be made, they would be insolent enough, and malicious and revengeful. But there is no danger, at present, and will be none until that event takes place. The weather has been sometimes bitterly cold, sometimes warm, sometimes rainy, and sometimes snowy, and the roads abominably hard and rough, so that this journey has been the most tedious I ever attempted. Our accommodations have been often very bad, but much better and cheaper than they would have been if we had taken the road from Peekskill to Morristown, where the army lies.

68. John Adams

Baltimore, 2 February 1777

LAST EVENING WE arrived safe in this town, after the longest journey and through the worst roads and the worst weather that I have ever experienced. My horses performed extremely well.

Baltimore is a very pretty town, situated on Patapsco River, which empties itself into the great bay of Chesapeake. The inhabitants are all good Whigs, having some time ago banished all the Tories from among them. The streets are very dirty and miry, but everything else is agreeable, except the monstrous prices of things. We cannot get a horse kept under a guinea a week. Our friends are well.

The Continental army is filling up fast, here and in Virginia. I pray that the Massachusetts may not fail of its quota in season. In this journey we have crossed four mighty rivers: Connecticut, Hudson, Delaware, and Susquehannah. The two first we crossed upon the ice, the two last in boats; the last we crossed a little above the place where it empties into Chesapeake Bay.

I think I have never been better pleased with any of our American States than with Maryland. We saw most excellent farms all along the road, and what was more striking to me, I saw more sheep and flax in Maryland than I ever saw in riding a like distance in any other State. We scarce passed a farm without seeing a fine flock of sheep, and scarce a house without seeing men or women dressing flax. Several times we saw women breaking and swingling this necessary article.

I have been to meeting and heard my old acquaintance, Mr. Allison, a worthy clergyman of this town, whom I have often seen in Philadelphia.

69. John Adams

Baltimore, 3 February 1777

THIS DAY HAS been observed in this place with exemplary decency and solemnity, in consequence of an appointment of the government, in observance of a recommendation of Congress, as a day of fasting. I went to the Presbyterian meeting, and heard Mr. Allison deliver a most pathetic and animating as well as pious, patriotic, and elegant discourse. I have seldom been better pleased or more affected with a sermon. The Presbyterian meeting-house in Baltimore stands upon a hill just at the back of the town, from whence we have a very fair prospect of the town and of the water upon which it stands, and of the country round it. Behind this eminence, which is the Beacon Hill of Baltimore, lies a beautiful meadow, which is entirely encircled by a stream of water. This most beautiful scene must be partly natural and partly artificial. Beyond the meadow and canal, you have a charming view of the country. Besides the meeting-house, there is upon this height a large and elegant Court House, as yet unfinished within, and a small church of England, in which an old clergyman officiates, Mr. Chase, father of Mr. Chase one of the delegates of Maryland, who, they say, is not so zealous a Whig as his son.

I shall take opportunities to describe this town and State more particularly to you hereafter. I shall inquire into their religion, their laws, their customs, their manners, their descent and education, their learning, their schools and colleges, and their morals. It was said of Ulysses, I think, that he saw the manners of many men and many cities; which is like to be my case, as far as American men and cities extend, provided Congress should continue in the rolling humor, which I hope they will not. I wish, however, that my mind was more at rest than it is, that I might be able to make more exact observation of men and things, as far as I go.

When I reflect upon the prospect before me, of so long an absence from all that I hold dear in this world, I mean, all that contributes to my private personal happiness, it makes me melancholy. When I think on your circumstances I am more so, and yet I rejoice at them in spite of all this melancholy. God Almighty's providence protect and bless you, and yours and mine.

70. John Adams

Baltimore, 7 February 1777

I AM AT LAST, after a great deal of difficulty, settled in comfortable quarters, but at an infinite expense. The price I pay for my board is more moderate than any other gentlemen give, excepting my colleagues, who are all in the same quarters and at the same rates, except Mr. Hancock, who keeps a house by himself. The prices of things here are much more intolerable than at Boston. The attempt of New England to regulate prices is extremely popular in Congress, who will recommend an imitation of it to the other States. For my own part I expect only a partial and a temporary relief from it, and I fear that after a time the evils will break out with greater violence. The water will flow with greater rapidity for having been dammed up for a time. The only radical cure will be to stop the emission of more paper, and to draw in some that is already out and devise means effectually to support the credit of the rest. To this end we must begin forthwith to tax the people as largely as the distressed circumstances of the country will bear. We must raise the interest from four to six per cent. We must, if possible, borrow silver and gold from abroad. We must, above all things, endeavor this winter to gain further advantages of the enemy, that our power may be in somewhat higher reputation than it is, or rather than it has been.

71. John Adams

Baltimore, 7 February 1777

I THINK IN some letter I sent you since I left Bethlehem I promised you a more particular account of that curious and remarkable town. When we first came in sight of the town we found a country better cultivated and more agreeably diversified with prospects of orchards and fields, groves and meadows, hills and valleys, than any we had seen. When we came into the town, we were directed to a public-house kept by a Mr. Johnson, which I think was the best inn I ever saw. It belongs, it seems, to the society, is furnished at their expense, and is kept for their profit or at their loss. Here you might find every accommodation that you could wish for yourself, your servants, and horses, and at no extravagant rates neither.

The town is regularly laid out, the streets straight and at right angles, like those in Philadelphia. It stands upon an eminence, and has a fine large brook flowing on one end of it, and the Lehigh, a branch of the Delaware, on the other. Between the town and the Lehigh are beautiful public gardens. They have carried the mechanical arts to greater perfection here than in any place which I have seen. They have a set of pumps which go by water, which force the water up through leaden pipes from the river to the top of the hill, near a hundred feet, and to the top of a little building in the shape of a pyramid or obelisk, which stands upon the top of the hill, and is twenty or thirty feet high. From this fountain water is conveyed in pipes to every part of the town. Upon the river they have a fine set of mills; the best grist mills and bolting mills that are anywhere to be found; the best fulling mills, an oil mill, a mill to grind bark for the tanyard, a dyeing house where all colors are dyed, machines for shearing cloth, etc.

There are three public institutions here of a very remarkable nature. One a society of the young men, another of the young women, and a third of the widows. There is a large building divided into many apartments, where the young men reside by themselves and carry on their several trades. They pay a rent to the society for their rooms and they pay for their board, and what they earn is their own. There is another large building appropriated in the same manner to the young women. There is a governess, a little like the lady abbess in some other institutions, who has the superintendence of the whole, and they have Elders. Each apartment has a number of young women who are vastly industrious, some spinning, some weaving, others employed in all the most curious works in linen, wool, cotton, silver and gold, silk and velvet. This institution displeased me much. Their dress was uniform and clean, but very inelegant. Their rooms were kept extremely warm with Dutch stoves, and the heat, the want of fresh air and exercise, relaxed the poor girls in such a manner as must, I think, destroy their health. Their countenances were languid and pale.

The society of widows is very similar. Industry and economy are remarkable in all these institutions. They showed us their Church, which is hung with pictures of our Saviour from his birth to his death, resurrection, and ascension. It is done with very strong colors and very violent passions, but not in a very elegant taste. The painter, who is still living in Bethlehem, but very old, has formerly been in Italy, the school of painting. They have a very good organ in their Church, of their own make. They have a public building on purpose for the reception of the dead, to which the corpse is carried as soon as it expires, where it lies until the time of sepulture.

Christian love is their professed object, but it is said they love money and make their public institutions subservient to the gratification of that passion. They suffer no lawsuits with one another, and as few as possible with other men. It is said that they now profess to be against war. They have a custom peculiar respecting courtship and marriage. The elders pick out pairs to be coupled together, who have no opportunity of conversing together more than once or twice before the knot is tied. The youth of the two sexes have very little conversation with one another before marriage.

Mr. Hassey, a very agreeable, sensible gentleman, who showed us the curiosities of the place, told me, upon inquiry, that they profess the Augsburg confession of faith, are Lutherans rather than Calvinists, distinguish between Bishops and Presbyters, but have no idea of the necessity of the uninterrupted succession, are very liberal and candid in their notions in opposition to bigotry, and live in charity with all denominations.

72. Abigail Adams

8 February 1777

BEFORE THIS TIME I fancy you at your journey's end. I have pitied
you. The season has been a continued cold. I have heard oftener from
you than I ever did in any of your former journeys. It has greatly
relieved my mind under its anxiety. I have received six letters from
you, and have the double pleasure of hearing you are well and that
your thoughts are often turned this way.

I have wrote once, by Major Rice. Two gentlemen set off for
Baltimore Monday or Tuesday, and have engaged to take this letter.
I feel under so many restraints when I sit down to write, that I scarcely
know what to say to you. The conveyance of letters is so precarious
that I shall not trust anything of consequence to them, until we have
more regular passes.

Indeed, very little of any consequence has taken place since you
left us. We seem to be in a state of tranquillity—rather too much so.
I wish there was a little more zeal to join the army.

Nothing new, but the regulating bill engrosses their attention. The
merchant scolds, the farmer growls, and every one seems wroth that
he cannot grind his neighbor.

We have a report here, said to come in two private letters, that a
considerable battle has taken place in Brunswick, in which we have
taken fifteen thousand prisoners. I cannot credit so good news. The
letters are said to be without date.

I beg you would write by every opportunity, and if you cannot
send so often as you used to, write and let them lie by till you make
a packet.

What has become of the Farmer. Many reports are abroad to his
disadvantage.

I feel as if you were gone to a foreign country. Philadelphia seemed close by; but now I hardly know how to reconcile myself to the thought that you are five hundred miles distant; but though distant, you are always near to   PORTIA

73. John Adams

Baltimore, 10 February 1777

FELL'S POINT, WHICH I mentioned in a letter this morning, has a considerable number of houses upon it. The shipping all lies now at this point. You have from it on one side a complete view of the harbor, and on the other a fine prospect of the town of Baltimore. You see the hill in full view, and the Court-house, the Church, and Meeting-house upon it. The Court-house makes a haughty appearance from this point. There is a fortification erected on this point, with a number of embrasures for cannon facing the Narrows which make the entrance into the harbor. At the Narrows they have a fort with a garrison in it.

It is now a month and a few days since I left you. I have heard nothing from you nor received a letter from the Massachusetts. I hope the post-office will perform better than it has done. I am anxious to hear how you do. I have in my mind a source of anxiety, which I never had before, since I became such a wanderer. You know what it is. Can't you convey to me in hieroglyphics, which no other person can comprehend, information which will relieve me? Tell me you are as well as can be expected. My duty to your papa and my mother. Love to brothers and sisters. Tell Betsey I hope she is married, though I want to throw the stocking. My respects to Mr. Shaw. Tell him he may be a Calvinist if he will, provided always that he preserves his candor, charity, and moderation. What shall I say of or to my children? What will they say to me for leaving them, their education, and fortune so much to the disposal of chance? May Almighty and all gracious Providence protect and bless them!

I have this day sent my resignation of a certain mighty office. It has relieved me from a burden which has a long time oppressed me. But I am determined that while I am ruining my constitution of mind and body, and running daily risks of my life and fortune, in defense of the independence of my country, I will not knowingly resign my own.

74. Abigail Adams

12 February 1777

MR. BROMFIELD WAS so obliging as to write me word that he designed a journey to the Southern States and would take particular care of a letter to you. I rejoice in so good an opportunity of letting you know that I am well as usual, but that I have not yet got reconciled to the great distance between us. I have many melancholy hours, when the best company is tiresome to me and solitude the greatest happiness I can enjoy.

I wait most earnestly for a letter to bring me the welcome tidings of your safe arrival. I hope you will be very particular and let me know how you are, after your fatiguing journey; how you are accommodated; how you like Maryland; what state of mind you find the Congress in. You know how little intelligence we received during your stay here with regard to what was passing there or in the army. We know no better now. All communication seems to be embarrassed. I got more knowledge from a letter written to you from your namesake, which I received since you left me, than I had before obtained since you left Philadelphia. I find by that letter that six Hessian officers, together with Colonel Campbell, had been offered in exchange for General Lee. I fear he receives very ill treatment. The terms were not complied with, as poor Campbell finds. He was much surprised when the officers went to take him and begged to know what he had been guilty of. They told him it was no crime of his own, but they were obliged, though reluctantly, to commit him to Concord Jail, in consequence of the ill treatment of General Lee. He then begged to know how long his confinement was to last. They told him that was impossible for

151

them to say, since it laid wholly in the power of General Howe to determine it.

By a vessel from Bilbao, we have accounts of the safe arrival of Dr. Franklin in France, ten days before she sailed. A French gentleman who came passenger says we may rely upon it that two hundred thousand Russians will be here in the spring.

A lethargy seems to have seized our countrymen. I hear no more of molesting or routing those troops at Newport than of attacking Great Britain. We just begin to talk of raising men for the standing army. I wish to know whether the reports may be credited of the Southern regiments being full.

You will write me by the bearer of this letter, to whose care you may venture to commit anything you have liberty to communicate. I have wrote to you twice before this; hope you have received them.

The children all desire to be remembered. So does your

PORTIA

75. John Adams

Baltimore, 15 February 1777

MR. HALL, BY whom this letter will be sent, will carry several letters to you, which have been written and delivered to him several days. He has settled his business agreeably. I have not received a line from the Massachusetts since I left it. Whether we shall return to Philadelphia soon or not, I cannot say. I rather conjecture it will not be long. You may write to me in Congress, and the letter will be brought me wherever I shall be.

I am settled now, agreeably enough, in my lodgings. There is nothing in this respect that lies uneasily upon my mind, except the most extravagant price which I am obliged to give for everything. My constituents will think me extravagant, but I am not. I wish I could sell or send home my horses, but I cannot. I must have horses and a servant, for Congress will be likely to remove several times, in the course of the ensuing year. I am impatient to hear from you, and most tenderly anxious for your health and happiness. I am also most affectionately solicitous for my dear children, to whom remember   Yours.

We long to hear of the formation of a new army. We shall lose the most happy opportunity of destroying the enemy this spring if we do not exert ourselves instantly. We have from New Hampshire a Colonel Thornton, a physician by profession, a man of humor. He has a large budget of droll stories with which he entertains company perpetually. I heard, about twenty or five-and-twenty years ago, a story of a physician in Londonderry, who accidentally met with one of our New England enthusiasts, called exhorters. The fanatic soon began to examine the Dr. concerning the articles of his faith and what he thought of original sin. "Why," says the Dr., "I satisfy myself about it in this manner. Either original sin is divisible or indivisible. If it is divisible, every descendant of Adam and Eve must have a part, and the share which falls to each individual at this day is so small a particle that I think it is not worth considering. If indivisible, then the whole quantity must have descended in a right line, and must now be possessed by one person only; and the chances are millions and millions and millions to one that that person is now in Asia or Africa, and that I have nothing to do with it." I told Thornton the story, and that I suspected him to be the man. He said he was. He belongs to Londonderry.

76. John Adams

Baltimore, 17 February 1777

IT WAS THIS day determined to adjourn, to-morrow week, to Philadelphia.

Howe, as you know my opinion always was, will repent his mad march through the Jerseys. The people of that Commonwealth begin to raise their spirits exceedingly and to be firmer than ever. They are actuated by resentment now, and resentment, coinciding with principle, is a very powerful motive.

I have got into the old routine of war office and Congress, which takes up my time in such a manner that I can scarce write a line. I have not time to think nor to speak. There is a United States Lottery abroad. I believe you had better buy a ticket and make a present of it to our four sweet ones, not forgetting the other sweet one. Let us try their luck. I hope they will be more lucky than their papa has ever been, or ever will be. I am as well as can be expected. How it happens I don't know, nor how long it will last. My disposition was naturally gay and cheerful, but the prospects I have ever had before me and these cruel times will make me melancholy. I, who would not hurt the hair of the head of any animal, I, who am always made miserable by the misery of every susceptible being that comes to my knowledge, am obliged to hear continual accounts of the barbarities, the cruel murders in cold blood even by the most tormenting ways of starving and freezing, committed by our enemies, and continued accounts of the deaths and diseases contracted by our people by their own imprudence. These accounts harrow me beyond description. These incarnate demons say in great composure, that "humanity is a Yankee virtue, but that they are governed by policy." Is there any policy on this side of hell that is inconsistent with humanity? I have no idea of it. I know of no policy, God is my witness, but this, piety, humanity, and honesty are the best policy. Blasphemy, cruelty, and villainy have prevailed and may again. But they won't prevail against America in this contest, because I find the more of them are employed the less they succeed.

77. John Adams

Baltimore, 21 February 1777

YESTERDAY I HAD the pleasure of dining with Mr. Purviance. There are two gentlemen of this name in Baltimore, Samuel and Robert, eminent merchants and in partnership. We had a brilliant company, the two Mrs. Purviances, the two Lees, the ladies of the two Colonels, R. H. and F., Mrs. Hancock and Miss Katy, and a young lady that belongs to the family. If this letter, like some other wise ones, should be intercepted, I suppose I shall be called to account for not adjusting the rank of these ladies a little better. Mr. Hancock, the two Colonels Lee, Colonel Whipple, Colonel Page, Colonel Ewing, the two Mr. Purviances, and a young gentleman. I fancy I have named all the company. How happy would this entertainment have been to me if I could, by a single volition, have transported one lady about five hundred miles. But alas! this is a greater felicity than falls to my share. We have voted to go to Philadelphia next week.

We have made General Lincoln a Continental Major-general. We shall make Colonel Glover a Brigadier. I sincerely wish we could hear more from General Heath. Many persons are extremely dissatisfied with numbers of the General officers of the highest rank. I don't mean the Commander-in-chief, his character is justly very high, but Schuyler, Putnam, Spencer, Heath, are thought by very few to be capable of the great commands they hold. We hear of none of their heroic deeds of arms. I wish they would all resign. For my part, I will vote upon the genuine principles of a republic for a new election of General officers annually, and every man shall have my consent to be left out who does not give sufficient proof of his qualifications.

157

I wish my lads were old enough. I would send every one of them into the army in some capacity or other. Military abilities and experience are a great advantage to any character.

78. John Adams

Philadelphia, 7 March 1777

THE PRESIDENT, WHO is just arrived from Baltimore, came in a few minutes ago and delivered me yours of February 8, which he found at Susquehanna River, on its way to Baltimore. It gives me great pleasure to find that you have received so many letters from me, although I knew they contained nothing of importance. I feel a restraint in writing, like that which you complain of, and am determined to go on trifling. However, the post now comes regularly, and I believe you may trust it. I am anxious and impatient to hear of the march of the Massachusetts soldiers for the new army. They are much wanted.

This city is a dull place in comparison of what it was. More than one half the inhabitants have removed into the country, as it was their wisdom to do. The remainder are chiefly Quakers, as dull as beetles. From these neither good is to be expected nor evil to be apprehended. They are a kind of neutral tribe, or the race of the insipids. Howe may possibly attempt this town, and a pack of sordid scoundrels, male and female, seem to have prepared their minds and bodies, houses and cellars, for his reception; but these are few, and more despicable in character than number. America will lose nothing by Howe's gaining this town. No such panic will be spread by it now as was spread by the expectation of it in December. However, if we can get together twenty thousand men by the first of April Mr. Howe will scarcely cross Delaware River this year. New Jersey may yet be his tomb, where he will have a monument very different from his brother's in Westminster Abbey.

I am very uneasy that no attempt is made at Rhode Island. There is but a handful left there, who might be made an easy prey. The few invalids who are left there are scattered over the whole island, which is eleven miles in length, and three or four wide. Are New England men such sons of sloth and fear as to lose this opportunity? We may possibly remove again from hence, perhaps to Lancaster or Reading. It is good to change place; it promotes health and spirits; it does good many ways; it does good to the place we remove from, as well as to that we remove to, and it does good to those who move. I long to be at home at the opening spring, but this is not my felicity. I am tenderly anxious for your health and for the welfare of the whole house.

79. John Adams

Philadelphia, 16 March 1777

THE SPRING ADVANCES very rapidly, and all nature will soon be clothed in her gayest robes. The green grass which begins to show itself here and there revives in my longing imagination my little farm and its dear inhabitants. What pleasure has not this vile war deprived me of? I want to wander in my meadows, to ramble over my mountains, and to sit, in solitude or with her who has all my heart, by the side of the brooks. These beautiful scenes would contribute more to my happiness than the sublime ones which surround me. I begin to suspect that I have not much of the grand in my composition. The pride and pomp of war, the continual sound of drums and fifes as well played as any in the world, the prancings and tramplings of the Light Horse, numbers of whom are paraded in the streets every day, have no charms for me. I long for rural and domestic scenes, for the warbling of birds and prattle of my children. Don't you think I am somewhat poetical this morning, for one of my years, and considering the gravity and insipidity of my employment? As much as I converse with sages and heroes, they have very little of my love or admiration. I should prefer the delights of a garden to the dominion of a world. I have nothing of Caesar's greatness in my soul. Power has not my wishes in her train. The Gods, by granting me health and peace and competence, the society of my family and friends, the perusal of my books, and the enjoyment of my farm and garden, would make me as happy as my nature and state will bear. Of that ambition which has power for its object, I don't believe I have a spark in my heart. There are other kinds of ambition of which I have a great deal.

I am now situated in a pleasant part of the town, in Walnut Street, on the south side of it, between Second and Third Streets, at the house of Mr. Duncan, a gentleman from Boston, who has a wife and three children. General Wolcot, of Connecticut, and Colonel Whipple, of Portsmouth, are with me in the same house. Mr. Adams has removed to Mrs. Cheesman's, in Fourth Street, near the corner of Market Street, where he has a curious group of company, consisting of characters as opposite as north and south. Ingersoll, the stamp man and Judge of Admiralty; Sherman, an old Puritan, as honest as an angel and as firm in the cause of American independence as Mount Atlas; and Colonel Thornton, as droll and funny as Tristram Shandy. Between the fun of Thornton, the gravity of Sherman, and the formal Toryism of Ingersoll, Adams will have a curious life of it. The landlady, too, who has buried four husbands, one tailor, two shoemakers, and Gilbert Tennent, and still is ready for a fifth, and well deserves him too, will add to the entertainment. Gerry and Lovell are yet at Miss Leonard's, under the auspices of Mrs. Yard. Mr. Hancock has taken a house in Chestnut Street, near the corner of Fourth Street, near the State House.

17 March

We this day received letters from Dr. Franklin and Mr. Deane. I am not at liberty to mention particulars, but in general, the intelligence is very agreeable. I am now convinced there will be a general war.

80. John Adams

Philadelphia, 28 March 1777

"A PLOT, A PLOT! a horrid plot! Mr. A.," says my barber, this morning. "It must be a plot, first, because there is British gold in it; second, because there is a woman in it; third, because there is a Jew in it; fourth, because I don't know what to make of it."

The barber means that a villain was taken up and examined yesterday, who appears, by his own confession, to have been employed, by Lord Howe and Jo. Galloway, to procure pilots to conduct the fleet up Delaware River and through the chevaux de frise. His confidant was a woman, who is said to be kept by a Jew. The fellow and the woman will suffer for their wickedness.

81. John Adams

I KNOW NOT the time when I have omitted to write you so long. I have received but three letters from you since we parted, and these were short ones. Do you write by the post? If you do, there must be some legerdemain. The post comes now constantly, once a week, and brings me newspapers, but no letters. I have ventured to write by the post, but whether my letters are received or not, I don't know. If you distrust the post, the Speaker or your uncle Smith will find frequent opportunities of conveying letters.

I never was more desirous of hearing from home, and never before heard so seldom. We have reports here not very favorable to the town of Boston. It is said that dissipation prevails, and that Toryism abounds and is openly avowed at the coffeehouses. I hope the reports are false. Apostasies in Boston are more abominable than in any other place. Toryism finds worse quarter here. A poor fellow detected here as a spy, employed, as he confesses, by Lord Howe and Mr. Galloway, to procure pilots for Delaware River and for other purposes, was this day at noon executed on the gallows, in the presence of an immense crowd of spectators. His name was James Molesworth. He has been Mayor's Clerk to three or four Mayors.

I believe you will think my letters very trifling; indeed, they are. I write in trammels. Accidents have thrown so many letters into the hands of the enemy, and they take such a malicious pleasure in exposing them, that I choose they should have nothing but trifles from me to expose. For this reason I never write anything of consequence from Europe, from Philadelphia, from camp, or anywhere else. If I could write freely, I would lay open to you the whole system of politics and war, and would delineate all the characters in either drama, as minutely, although I could not do it so elegantly, as Tully did in his letters to Atticus.

We have letters, however, from France by a vessel in at Portsmouth. Of her important cargo you have heard. There is news of very great importance in the letters, but I am not at liberty. The news, however, is very agreeable.